Brazilian Tales

Joaquim Maria Machado de Assis

Translator: Isaac Goldberg

Contents

BRAZILIAN TALES

BY

Joaquim Maria Machado de Assis

Translator: Isaac Goldberg

SOME INFORMAL PRELIMINARY REMARKS

The noted Brazilian critic, Jose Verissimo, in a short but important essay on the deficiencies of his country's letters, has expressed serious doubt as to whether there exists a genuinely Brazilian literature. "I do not know," he writes, "whether the existence of an entirely independent literature is possible without an entirely independent language." In this sense Verissimo would deny the existence of a Swiss, or a Belgian, literature. In this sense, too, it was no doubt once possible, with no small measure of justification, to deny the existence of an American, as distinguished from an English, literature. Yet, despite the subtle psychic bonds that link identity of speech to similarity of thought, the environment (which helps to shape pronunciation as well as vocabulary and the language itself) is, from the standpoint of literature, little removed from language as a determining factor. Looking at the question, however, from the purely linguistic standpoint, it is important to remember that the Spanish of Spanish America is more different from the parent tongue than is the English of this country from that of the mother nation. Similar changes have taken place in the Portuguese spoken in Brazil. Yet who would now pretend, on the basis of linguistic similarity, to say that there is no United States literature as distinguished from English literature? After all, is it not national life, as much as national language, that makes literature? And by an inversion of Verissimo's standard may we not come face to face with a state of affairs in which different literatures exist within the same tongue? Indeed, is not such a conception as the "great American novel" rendered quite futile in the United States by the fact that from the literary standpoint we are several countries rather than one?

The question is largely academic. At the same time it is interesting to notice the more assertive standpoint lately adopted by the charming Mexican poet, Luis G. Urbina, in his recent "La Vida Literaria de Mexico," where, without undue national pride he claims the right to use the adjective Mexican in qualifying the letters of his remarkable country. Urbina shows that different physiological and psychological types have been produced in his part of the New World; why, then, should the changes stop there? Nor have they ceased at that point, as Senor Urbina's delightful and informative book reveals. So, too, whatever the merits of the academic question involved, a book like Alencar's "Guarany," for instance, could not have been written outside of Brazil; neither could Verissimo's own "Scenes from Amazon Life."

II.

Brazilian literature has been divided into four main periods. The first extends from the age of discovery and exploration to the middle of the eighteenth century; the second includes the second half of the eighteenth century; the third comprises the years of the nineteenth century up to 1840, while that date inaugurates the triumph of Romanticism over pseudo-Classicism. Romanticism, as in other countries, gave way in turn to realism and various other movements current in those turbulent decades. Sometimes the changes came not as a natural phase of literary evolution, but rather as the consequence of pure imitation. Thus, Verissimo tells us, Symbolism, in Brazil, was a matter of intentional parroting, in many cases unintelligent. It did not correspond to a movement of reaction,--mystical, sensualist, individualist, socialistic or anarchistic,--as in Europe.

Two chief impulses were early present in Brazilian letters: that of Portuguese literature and that of the Jesuit colleges. At the time of the discovery of Brazil only Italy, Spain, France and Portugal possessed a literary life. Portugal, indeed, as the Brazilian critic points out, was then in its golden period. It boasted chroniclers like Fernao Lopes, novelists like Bernardim Ribeiro, historians like Joao de Barros, and dramatists of the stamp of Gil Vicente. The Jesuit colleges, too, were followed by other orders, spreading Latin culture and maintaining communication between the interior and the important centers. It is natural, then, that early letters in Brazil should have been Portuguese not only in language, but in inspiration, feeling and spirit. Similarly, we find the early intellectual dependence of the Spanish American countries upon Spain, even as later both the Spanish and the Portuguese writers of

America were to be influenced greatly by French literature. "Brazilian poetry," says Verissimo in the little essay already referred to, "was already in the seventeenth century superior to Portuguese verse." He foresaw a time when it would outdistance the mother country. But Brazilian literature as a whole, he found, lacked the perfect continuity, the cohesion, the unity of great literatures, chiefly because it began as Portuguese, later turned to east (particularly France) and only then to Brazil itself. In the early days it naturally lacked the solidarity that comes from easy communication between literary centers. This same lack of communication was in a sense still true at the time he wrote his essay. The element of communicability did exist during the Romantic period (1835-1860), whereupon came influences from France, England, Italy, and even Germany, and letters were rapidly denationalized. What was thus needed and beneficial from the standpoint of national culture prejudiced the interests of national literature, says Verissimo. He finds, too, that there is too little originality and culture among Brazilian writers, and that their work lacks sincerity and form (1899). Poetry was too often reduced to the love of form while fiction was too closely copied from the French, thus operating to stifle the development of a national dramatic literature. Excessive preoccupation with politics and finance (where have we heard that complaint elsewhere?) still further impeded the rise of a truly native literature.

Perhaps Verissimo's outlook was too pessimistic; he was an earnest spirit, unafraid to speak his mind and too much a lover of truth to be misled by a love of his country into making exaggerated claims for works by his countrymen. We must not forget that he was here looking upon Brazilian letters as a whole; in other essays by him we discover that same sober spirit, but he is alive to the virtues of his fellow writers as well as to their failings.

It is with the prose of the latest period in Brazilian literature that we are here concerned. From the point of view of the novel and tale Brazil shares with Argentina, Columbia, Chile and Mexico the leadership of the Latin-American republics[1]. If Columbia, in Jorge Isaacs' *Maria*, can show the novel best known to the rest of the world, and Chile, in such a figure as Alberto Blest-Gana (author of *Martin Rivas*

1   I am aware of the recent objection to this term (See my
      Studies in Spanish American Literature, pp. 233-237), but no
      entirely satisfactory substitute has been advanced.

and other novels) boasts a "South American Balzac," Brazil may point to more than one work of fiction that Is worthy of standing beside *Maria*, *Martin Rivas* or Jose Marmol's exciting tale of love and adventure, *Amalia*. The growing Importance of Brazil as a commercial nation, together with a corresponding increase of interest in the study of Portuguese (a language easily acquired by all who know Spanish) will have the desirable effect of making known to the English reading public a selection of works deserving of greater recognition.

Just to mention at random a few of the books that should in the near future be known to American readers, either in the original or through the medium of translations, I shall recall some of the names best known to Brazilians in connection with the modern tale and novel. If there be anything lacking in the array of modern writers it is a certain broad variety of subject and treatment to which other literatures have accustomed us.

It is not to be wondered at that in surroundings such as the Amazon affords an "Indian" school of literature should have arisen. We have an analogous type of fiction in United States literature, old and new, produced by similar causes. Brazilian "Indianism" reached its highest point perhaps in Jose Alencar's famous *Guarany*, which won for its author national reputation and achieved unprecedented success. From the book was made a libretto that was set to music by the Brazilian composer, Carlos Gomez. The story is replete with an intensity of life and charming descriptions that recall the pages of Chateaubriand, and its prose often verges upon poetry in its idealization of the Indian race. Of the author's other numerous works *Iracema* alone approaches *Guarany* in popularity. The dominant note of the author, afterward much repeated in the literary history of his nation, is the essential goodness and self-abnegation of the national character.

Alfred d'Escragnolle Taunay (1843-1899) is among the most important of Brazil's novelists. Born at Rio de Janeiro of noble family he went through a course in letters and science, later engaging in the campaign of Paraguay. He took part in the retreat of La Laguna, an event which he has enshrined in one of his best works, first published in French under the title *La Retraite de la Laguna*. He served also as secretary to Count d'Eu, who commanded the Brazilian army, and later occupied various political offices, rising to the office of senator in 1886. His list of works is too numerous to mention in a fragmentary introduction of this nature; chief among them stands *Innocencia*; a sister tale, so to speak, to Isaacs's **Maria**. According to Verissimo, *Innocencia* is one of the country's few genuinely original novels. It has been called, by Merou (1900), "the best novel written in South America by a South American," a compliment later paid by Guglielmo Ferrero to Graca Aranha's **Canaan**. Viscount Taunay's famous work has been translated into French twice, once into English, Italian, German, Danish, and even Japanese.

The scene is laid in the deserted Matto Grosso, a favorite background of the author's. Innocencia is all that her name implies, and dwells secluded with her father, who is a miner, her negress slave Conga, and her Caliban-like dwarf Tico, who loves Innocencia, the Miranda of this district. Into Innocencia's life comes the itinerant physician, Cirino de Campos, who is called by her father to cure her of the fever. Cirino is her Ferdinand; they make love in secret, for she is meant by paternal arrangement for a mere brute of a mule driver, Manacao by name. Innocencia vows herself to Cirino, when the mule-driver comes to enforce his prior claim; the father, bound by his word of honor, sides with the primitive lover. The tragedy seems fore-ordained, for Innocencia makes spirited resistance, while Manacao avenges himself by killing the doctor. A comic figure of a German scientist adds humor and a certain poignant irony to the tale. Such a bare outline conveys nothing of the mysterious charm of the original, nor of its poetic atmosphere. Comparing *Innocencia* with what has been termed its sister work, *Maria*, I believe that *Maria* is the better tale of the two, although there is much to be said for both. The point need not be pressed. The heroine of *Maria* is more a woman, less a child than Innocencia, hence the fate of the Spanish girl is tragic where that of the other maiden is merely pitiful. *Innocencia*, on the other hand, is stouter in texture. In *Maria* there is no love struggle; the struggle is with life and circumstance; in *Innocencia* there is not only the element of rivalry in love, but in addition there is the rigid parent who sternly, and at last murderously, opposes the natural desires of a child whom he has promised to another. Where *Maria* is idyllic, poetic, flowing smoothing along the current of a realism tempered by sentimentalism, *Innocencia* (by no means devoid of poetry) is romantic, melodramatic, rushing along turbulently to the outcome in a death as violent as Maria's is peaceful. There is in each book a similar importance of the background. In *Innocencia* the "point of honor" is quite as strong and vindictive as in any play of the Spanish Golden Age. *Maria* shares with *Innocencia* relieving touches of humor and excellent pages of character description.

Taunay's *O Encilhamento* is a violent antithesis to the work just considered. Here the politician speaks. In passages of satire that becomes so acrimonious at times as to indicate real personages, the wave of speculation that swept Argentina and Brazil is analyzed and held up to scorn. The novel is really a piece of historical muck-raking and was long an object of resentment in the republic.

Everything from Taunay's pen reveals a close communion with nature, an intimate understanding of the psychology of the vast region's inhabitants. His shorter tales, which I hope later to present to the English-reading public, reveal these powers at their best. Now it is a soldier who goes to war, only, like a military Enoch Arden, to return and find his sweetheart in another's arms; now it is a clergyman, "the vicar of sorrows," who, in the luxuriant environment of his charge suffers the tortures of carnal temptations, with the spirit at last triumphant over the flesh. Whatever of artifice there is in these tales is overcome, one of his most sympathetic critics tells us, by the poetic sincerity of the whole. Taunay, too, has been likened to Pierre Loti for his exotic flavor. In *Yerece a Guana* we have a miniature *Innocencia*. Yerece and Alberto Monteiro fall in love and marry. The latter has been cured, at the home of Yerece, of swamp fever. The inevitable, however, occurs, and Montero hears the call of civilization. The marriage, according to the custom of the tribe into which Montero has wed, is dissolved by the man alone. He returns to his old life and she dies of grief.

A work that may stand beside *Innocencia* and Verissimo's *Scenes from Amazon Life* as a successful national product is Inglez de Sousa's *O Missionario*. Antonio de Moraes, in this story, is not so strong in will as Taunay's vicar of sorrows. Antonio is a missionary "with the vocation of a martyr and the soul of an apostle," on duty in the tropics. The voluptuous magnetism of the Amazon seizes his body. Slowly, agonizingly, but surely he succumbs to the enchantment, overpowered by the life around him.

Since Machado de Assis (who should precede Azevedo) and Coelho Netto (who should follow him, if strict chronological order were being observed) are both referred to in section three, which deals particularly with the authors represented in this sample assortment of short tales, they are here omitted.

With the appearance of *O Mulato* by Aluizio Azevedo (1857-1912), the literature of Brazil, prepared for such a reorientation by the direct influence of the great Portuguese, Eca de Queiroz, and Emile Zola, was definitely steered toward naturalism. "In Aluizio Azevedo," says Benedicto Costa, "one finds neither the poetry of Jose de Alencar, nor the delicacy,--I should even say, archness--of Macedo, nor the sentimental preciosity of Taunay, nor the subtle irony of Machado de Assis. His phrase is brittle, lacking lyricism, tenderness, dreaminess, but it is dynamic, energetic, expressive, and, at times, sensual to the point of sweet delirium."

O Mulato, though it was the work of a youth in his early twenties, has been acknowledged as a solid, well-constructed example of Brazilian realism. There is a note of humor, as well as a lesson in criticism, in the author's anecdote (told in his foreword to the fourth edition) about the provincial editor who advised the youthful author to give up writing and hire himself out on a farm. This was all the notice he received from his native province, Maranhao. Yet Azevedo grew to be one of the few Brazilian authors who supported himself by his pen.

When Brazilian letters are better known in this nation, among Azevedo's work we should be quick to appreciate such a pithy book as the *Livro de uma Sogra*,--the Book of a Mother-in-Law. And when the literature of these United States is at last (if ever, indeed!) released from the childish, hypocritical, Puritanic inhibitions forced upon it by quasi official societies, we may even relish, from among Azevedo's long shelf of novels, such a sensuous product as *Cortico*.

I have singled out, rather arbitrarily it must be admitted, a few of the characteristic works that preceded the appearance of Graca Aranha's *Canaan*, the novel that was lifted into prominence by Guglielmo Ferrero's fulsome praise of it as the "great American novel."[2] For South America, no less than North, is hunting that literary will o' the wisp. Both *Maria* and *Innocencia* have been mentioned for that honor.

There is a distinct basis for comparison between *Innocencia* and the more famous Spanish American tale from Colombia; between these and *Canaan*, however, there is little similarity, if one overlook the poetic atmosphere that glamours all three. Aranha's masterpiece is of far broader conception than the other two; it

---

2   Issued, in English (1920) by the publishers of this book.

adds to their lyricism an epic sweep inherent in the subject and very soon felt in the treatment. It is, in fact, a difficult novel to classify, impregnated as it is with a noble idealism, yet just as undoubtedly streaked with a powerful realism. This should, however, connote no inept mingling of genres; the style seems to be called for by the very nature of the vast theme--that moment at which the native and the immigrant strain begin to merge in the land of the future--the promised land that the protagonists are destined never to enter, even as Moses himself, upon Mount Nebo in the land of Moab, beheld Canaan and died in the throes of the great vision.

Canaan is of those novels that centre about an enthralling idea. The type which devotes much attention to depictions of life and customs, to discussions upon present realities and ultimate purposes, is perhaps more frequent among Spanish and Portuguese Americans than among our own readers who are apt to be over-insistent in their demands for swift, visible action. Yet, in the hands of a master, it possesses no less interest than the more obvious type of fiction, for ideas possess more life than the persons who are moved by them.

The idea that carries Milkau from the Old World to the New is an ideal of human brotherhood, high purpose and dissatisfaction with the old, degenerate world. In the State of Espirito Santo, where the German colonists are dominant, he plans a simple life that shall drink inspiration in the youth of a new, virgin continent. He falls in with another German, Lentz, whose outlook upon life is at first the very opposite to Milkau's blend of Christianity and a certain liberal socialism. The strange milieu breeds in both an intellectual langour that vents itself in long discussions, in breeding contemplation, mirages of the spirit. Milkau is gradually struck with something wrong in the settlement. Little by little it begins to dawn upon him that something of the Old-World hypocrisy, fraud and insincerity, is contaminating this supposedly virgin territory. Here he discovers no paradise a la Rousseau--no natural man untainted by the ills of civilization. Graft is as rampant as in any district of the world across the sea; cruelty is as rife. His pity is aroused by the plight of Mary, a destitute servant who is betrayed by the son of her employers. Not only does the scamp desert her when she most needs his protection and acknowledgment, but he is silent when his equally vicious parents drive her forth to a life of intense hardship. She is spurned at every door and reduced to beggary. Her child is born under the most distressing circumstances, and under conditions that strike the note of horror the infant is slain before her very eyes while she gazes helplessly on.

Mary is accused of infanticide, and since she lacks witnesses, she is placed in a very difficult position. Moreover, the father of her child bends every effort to loosen the harshest measures of the community against her, whereupon Milkau, whose heart is open to the sufferings of the universe, has another opportunity to behold man's inhumanity to woman. His pity turns to what pity is akin to; he effects her release from jail, and together they go forth upon a journey that ends in the delirium of death. The promised land had proved a mirage--at least for the present. And it is upon this indecisive note that the book ends.

Ferrero's introduction, though short, is substantial, and to the point. It is natural that he should have taken such a liking to the book, for Aranha's work is of intense interest to the reader who looks for psychological power, and Ferrero himself is the exponent of history as psychology rather than as economic materialism. "The critics," he says, "will judge the literary merits of this novel. As a literary amateur I will point out among its qualities the beauty of its style and its descriptions, the purity of the psychological analysis, the depth of the thoughts and the reflections of which the novel is full, and among its faults a certain disproportion between the different parts of the book and an ending which is too vague, indefinite and unexpected. But its literary qualities seem to me to be of secondary importance to the profound and incontrovertible idea that forms the kernel of the book. Here in Europe we are accustomed to say that modern civilization develops itself in America more freely than in Europe, for in the former country it has not to surmount the obstacle of an older society, firmly established, as in the case of the latter. Because of this, we call America 'the country of the young,' and we consider the New World as the great force which decomposes the old European social organization." That idea is, as Ferrero points out, an illusion due to distance. He points out, too, that here is everywhere "an old America struggling against a new one and, this is very curious, the new America, which upsets traditions, is formed above all by the European immigrants who seek a place for themselves in the country of their adoption, whereas the real Americans represent the conservative tendencies. Europe exerts on American society--through its emigrants--the same dissolving action which America exerts--through its novelties and its example--on the old civilization of Europe." The point is very well taken, and contains the germ of a great novel of the United States.

And just as **Canaan** stands by itself in Brazilian literature, so might such a novel achieve preeminence in our own.

Ferrero is quite right in indicating the great non-literary importance of the novel, though not all readers will agree with him as to the excessive vagueness of the end. Hardly any other type of ending would have befitted a novel that treats of transition, of a landscape that dazzles and enthralls, of possibilities that founder, not through the malignance of fate, but through the stupidity of man. There is an epic swirl to the finale that reminds one of the disappearance of an ancient deity in a pillar of dust. For an uncommon man like Milkau an uncommon end was called for. Numerous questions are touched upon in the course of the leisurely narrative, everywhere opening up new vistas of thought; for Aranha is philosophically, critically inclined; his training is cosmopolitan, as his life has been; he knows the great Germans, Scandinavians, Belgians and Russians; his native exuberance has been tempered by a serenity that is the product of European influence. He is some fifty-two years of age, has served his nation at Christiania as minister, at the Hague, and as leader in the Allied cause. He is, therefore, an acknowledged and proven spokesman. The author of **Canaan** has done other things, among which this book, which has long been known in French and Spanish, stands out as a document that marks an epoch in Brazilian history as well as a stage in Brazilian literature. Whether it is "the" great American novel is of interest only to literary politicians and pigeon-holers; it is "a" great novel, whether of America or Europe, and that suffices for the lover of belles lettres.

III.

In considering the work of such writers as these and the authors represented in this little pioneer volume one should bear continually in mind the many handicaps under which authorship labors in Portuguese and Spanish America: a small reading public, lack of publishers, widespread prevalence of illiteracy, instability of politics. Under the circumstances it is not so much to be wondered at that the best work is of such a high average as that it was done at all. For in nations where education is so limited and illiteracy so prevalent the manifold functions which in more highly developed nations are performed by many are perforce done by a few. Hence the spectacle in the new Spanish and Portuguese world, as in the old, of men and women who are at once journalists, novelists, dramatists, politicians, soldiers, poets and what not else. Such a versatility, often joined to a literary prolixity, no doubt serves to lower the artistic worth of works produced under such conditions.

In connection with the special character of the tales included in the present sample of modern Brazilian short stories,--particularly those by Machado de Assis and Medeiros e Albuquerque--it is interesting to keep in mind the popularity of Poe and Hawthorne in South America. The introspection of these men, as of de Maupassant and kindred spirits, appeals to a like characteristic of the Brazilians. Such inner seeking, however, such preoccupation with psychological problems, does not often, in these writers, reach the point or morbidity which we have become accustomed to expect in the novels and tales of the Russians. Stories like *The Attendant's Confession* are written with a refinement of thought as well as of language. They are not, as so much of Brazilian literature must perforce seem to the stranger's mind, exotic. They belong to the letters of the world by virtue of the human appeal of the subject and the mastery of their treatment.

Chief among the writers here represented stands Joaquim Maria Machado de Assis. (1839-1908). Born in Rio de Janeiro of poor parents he was early beset with difficulties. He soon found his way into surroundings where his literary tastes were awakened and where he came into contact with some of the leading spirits of the day. The noted literary historians of his country, Sylvio Romero and Joao Ribeiro (in their *Compendio de Historia da Litteratura Brazileira*) find the writing of his first period of little value. The next decade, from his thirtieth to his fortieth year, is called transitional. With the year 1879, however, Machado de Assis began a long phase of maturity that was to last for thirty years. It was during this fruitful period that *Memorias Postumas de Braz Cubas, Quincas Borbas, Historias Sem Data, Dom Casmurro, Varias Historias* and other notable works were produced. The three tales by Machado de Assis in this volume are translated from his *Varias Historias*. That same bitter-sweet philosophy and gracious, if penetrating, irony which inform these tales are characteristic of his larger romances. Four volumes of poetry sustain his reputation as poet. He is found, by Romero and Ribeiro, to be very correct and somewhat cold in his verse. He took little delight in nature and lacked the passionate, robust temperament that projects itself upon pages of ardent beauty. In the best of his prose works, however, he penetrates as deep as any of his countrymen into the abyss of the human soul.

The judgment of Verissimo upon Machado de Assis differs somewhat from that of his distinguished compatriots. Both because of the importance of Machado de Assis to Brazilian literature, and as an insight into Verissimo's delightful critical style, I translate somewhat at length from that writer.

"With *Varias Historias*," he says in his studies of Brazilian letters, "Sr. Machado de Assis published his fifteenth volume and his fifth collection of tales ... To say that in our literature Machado de Assis is a figure apart, that he stands with good reason first among our writers of fiction, that he possesses a rare faculty of assimilation and evolution which makes him a writer of the second Romantic generation, always a contemporary, a modern, without on this account having sacrificed anything to the latest literary fashion or copied some brand-new aesthetic, above all conserving his own distinct, singular personality ... is but to repeat what has been said many times already. All these judgments are confirmed by his latest book, wherein may be noted the same impeccable correctness of language, the same firm grasp upon form, the same abundancy, force and originality of thought that make of him the only thinker among our writers of fiction, the same sad, bitter irony ...

"After this there was published another book by Sr. Machado de Assis, *Yaya Garcia*. Although this is really a new edition, we may well speak of it here since the first, published long before, is no longer remembered by the public. Moreover, this book has the delightful and honest charm of being in the writer's first manner.

"But let us understand at once, this reference to Machado de Assis's first manner. In this author more than once is justified the critical concept of the unity of works displayed by the great writers. All of Machado de Assis is practically present in his early works; in fact, he did not change, he scarcely developed. He is the most individual, the most personal, the most 'himself' of our writers; all the germs of this individuality that was to attain in *Braz Cubas*, in *Quincas Borbas*, in the *Papeis Avulsos* and in *Varias Historias* its maximum of virtuosity, may be discovered in his first poems and in his earliest tales. His second manner, then, of which these books are the best example, is only the logical, natural, spontaneous development of his first, or rather, it is the first manner with less of the romantic and more of the critical tendencies ... The distinguishing trait of Machado de Assis is that he is, in our literature, an artist and a philosopher. Up to a short time ago he was the only one answering to such a description. Those who come after him proceed consciously and unconsciously from him, some of them being mere worthless imitators. In this genre, if I am not misemploying that term, he remained without a peer. Add that this philosopher is a pessimist by temperament and by conviction, and you will have as complete a characterization as it is possible to design of so strong and complex a figure as his in two strokes of the pen.

"*Yaya Garcia*, like *Resurreicao* and *Helena*, is a romantic account, perhaps the most romantic written by the author. Not only the most romantic, but perhaps the most emotional. In the books that followed it is easy to see how the emotion is, one might say, systematically repressed by the sad irony of a disillusioned man's realism." Verissimo goes on to imply that such a work as this merits comparison with the humane books of Tolstoi. But this only on the surface. "For at bottom, it contains the author's misanthropy. A social, amiable misanthropy, curious about everything, interested in everything,--what is, in the final analysis, a way of loving mankind without esteeming it...

"The excellency with which the author of *Yaya Garcia* writes our language is proverbial ... The highest distinction of the genius of Machado de Assis in Brazilian literature is that he is the only truly universal writer we possess, without ceasing on that account to be really Brazilian."

When the Brazilian Academy of letters was founded in 1897, Machado de Assis was unanimously elected president and held the position until his death. Oliveira Lima, who lectured at Harvard during the college season of 1915-1916, and who is himself one of the great intellectual forces of contemporary Brazil, has written of Machado de Assis: "By his extraordinary talent as writer, by his profound literary dignity, by the unity of a life that was entirely devoted to the cult of intellectual beauty, and by the prestige exerted about him by his work and by his personality, Machado de Assis succeeded, despite a nature that was averse to acclaim and little inclined to public appearance, in being considered and respected as the first among his country's men-of-letters: the head, if that word can denote the idea, of a youthful literature which already possesses its traditions and cherishes above all its glories ... His life was one of the most regulated and peaceful after he had given up active journalism, for like so many others, he began his career as a political reporter, paragrapher and dramatic critic."

Coelho Netto (Anselmo Ribas, 1864-) is known to his countrymen as a professor of literature at Rio de Janeiro. His career has covered the fields of journalism, politics, education and fiction. Although his work is of uneven worth, no doubt because of his unceasing productivity, he is reckoned by so exacting a critic as Verissimo as one of Brazil's most important writers,--one of the few, in fact, that will be remembered by posterity. Among his best liked stories are "Death," "The Federal Capital," "Paradise," "The Conquest," and "Mirage." Netto's short stories are very popular; at one time every other youth in Brazil was imitating his every mannerism. He is particularly felicitous in his descriptions of tropical nature, which teem with glowing life and vivid picturesqueness.

Coelho Netto is considered one of the chief writers of the modern epoch. "He is really an idealist," writes Verissimo, "but an idealist who has drunk deeply of the strong, dangerous milk of French naturalism." He sees nature through his soul rather than his eyes, and has been much influenced by the mystics of Russia, Germany and Scandinavia. His style is derived chiefly from the Portuguese group of which Eca de Queiroz is the outstanding figure, and his language has been much affected by this attachment to the mother country. His chief stylistic quality is an epic note, tempered by a sentimental lyricism.

In his book *Le Roman au Bresil* (The Novel in Brazil, which I believe the author himself translated from the original Portuguese into French) Benedicto Costa, after considering Aluizio Azevedo as the exponent of Brazilian naturalism and the epicist of the race's sexual instincts, turns to Coelho Netto's neo-romanticism, as the "eternal praise of nature, the incessant, exaggerated exaltation of the landscape..." In Netto he perceives the most Brazilian, the least European of the republic's authors. "One may say of him what Taine said of Balzac: 'A sort of literary elephant, capable of bearing prodigious burdens, but heavy-footed.' And in fact ... he reveals a great resemblance to Balzac,--a relative Balzac, for the exclusive use of a people,--but a Balzac none the less."

Despite his lack of ideas, his mixture of archaisms, neologisms, his exuberance, his slow development of plots, his lack of proportion (noticeable, naturally, in his longer works rather than in his short fiction) he stands pre-eminent as a patron of the nation's intellectual youth and as the romancer of its opulent imagination.

Medeiros e Albuquerque (1867-) is considered by some critics to be the leading exponent in the country of "the manner of de Maupassant, enveloped by an indefinable atmosphere that seems to bring back Edgar Allan Poe." He has been director-general of public instruction in Rio de Janeiro, professor at the Normal School and the National School of Fine Arts, and also a deputy from Pernambuco. With the surprising versatility of so many South Americans he has achieved a reputation as poet, novelist, dramatist, publicist, journalist and philosopher.

IV.

The part that women have played in the progress of the South American republics is as interesting as it is little known. The name of the world's largest river--the Amazon, or more exactly speaking, the Amazons--stands as a lasting tribute to the bravery of the early women whom the explorer Orellana encountered during his conquest of the mighty flood[3]. For he named the river in honor of the tribes' fighting heroines. Centuries later, when one by one the provinces of South America rose to liberate themselves from the Spanish yoke, the women again played a noble part in the various revolutions. The statue in Colombia to Policarpa Salavarieta is but a symbol of South American gratitude to a host of women who fought side by side with their husbands during the trying days of the early nineteenth century. One of them, Manuela la Tucumana, was even made an officer in the Argentine army.

If women, however, have enshrined themselves in the patriotic annals of the Southern republics, they have shown that they are no less the companions of man in the more or less agreeable arts of peace. When one considers the great percentage of illiteracy that still prevails in Southern America, and the inferior intellectual position which for years has been the lot of woman particularly in the Spanish and

---

3   This derivation of the river's name is by many considered
    fanciful. A more likely source of the designation is the Indian
    word "Amassona," i.e., boat-destroyer, referring to the tidal
    phenomenon known as "bore" or "proroca," which sometimes uproots
    tress and sweeps away whole tracts of land.

Portuguese nations, it is surprising that woman's prominence in the literary world should be what it is.

The name of the original seventeenth century spirit known as Sor Ines de la Cruz (Mexico) is part of Spanish literature. Only recently has she been indicated as her nation's first folklorist and feminist! Her poems have found their way into the anthologies of universal poesy. The most distinguished Spanish poetess of the nineteenth century, Gertrudis Gomez de Avellaneda, was a Cuban by birth, going later to Spain, where she was readily received as one of the nation's leading literary lights. Her poetry is remarkable for its virile passion; her novel "Sab" has been called the Spanish "Uncle Tom's Cabin" for its stirring protest against slavery and its idealization of the oppressed race. She was a woman of striking beauty, yet so vigorous in her work and the prosecution of it that one facetious critic was led to exclaim, "This woman is a good deal of a man!"

But South America has its native candidate for the title of Spanish "Uncle Tom's Cabin," and this, too, is the work of a woman. Clorinda Matto's "Aves Sin Nido" (Birds Without a Nest) is by one of Peru's most talented women, and exposes the disgraceful exploitation of the Indians by conscienceless citizens and priests who had sunk beneath their holy calling. It seems, indeed, that fiction as a whole in Peru has been left to the pens of the women. Such names as Joana Manuele Girriti de Belzu, Clorinda Matto and Mercedes Cabello de Carbonero stand for what is best in the South American novel. The epoch in which these women wrote (late nineteenth century) and the natural feminine tendency to put the house in order (whether it be the domestic or the national variety) led to such stories as Carbonero's "Las Consequencias," "El Conspirador" and "Blanca Sol." The first of these is an indictment of the Peruvian vice of gambling; the second throws an interesting light upon the origin of much of the internal strife of South America, and portrays a revolution brought on by the personal disappointment of a politician. "Blanca Sol" has been called a Peruvian "Madame Bovary."

Although Brazil has not yet produced any Amazons of poetry or fiction to stand beside such names as Sor Ines de la Cruz or Gertrudis Gomez de Avallaneda, it has contributed some significant names to the women writers of Latin America. Not least among these is Carmen Dolores (Emilia Moncorvo Bandeira de Mello) who was born in 1852 at Rio de Janeiro and died in 1910, after achieving a wide reputation in the field of the short story, novel and feuilleton. In addition to these activities she made herself favorably known in the press of Rio, Sao Paulo and Pernambuco. Her career started with the novel *Confession*. Other works are *The Struggle*, *A Country Drama*, and *Brazilian Legends*. The story in this volume is taken from a collection entitled *The Complex Soul*.

*   *   *   *   *   *   *

The present selection of tales makes no pretense at completeness, finality or infallibility of choice. This little book is, so to speak, merely a modest sample-case. Some of the tales first appeared, in English, in the *Boston Evening Transcript* and the *Stratford Journal* (Boston), to which organs I am indebted for permission to reprint them.

ISAAC GOLDBERG.

Roxbury, Mass.

THE ATTENDANT'S CONFESSION
By Joaquim Maria Machado de Assis

First President of the Brazilian Academy of Letters

So it really seems to you that what happened to me in 1860 is worth while writing down? Very well. I'll tell you the story, but on the condition that you do not divulge it before my death. You'll not have to wait long--a week at most; I am a marked man.

I could have told you the story of my whole life, which holds many other interesting details: but for that there would be needed time, courage and paper. There is plenty of paper, indeed, but my courage is at low ebb, and as to the time that is yet left me, it may be compared to the life of a candle-flame. Soon tomorrow's sun will rise--a demon sun as impenetrable as life itself. So goodbye, my dear sir; read this and bear me no ill will; pardon me those things that will appear evil to you and do not complain too much if there is exhaled a disagreeable odor which is not exactly that of the rose. You asked me for a human document. Here it is. Ask me for neither the empire of the Great Mogul nor a photograph of the Maccabees; but request, if you will, my dead man's shoes, and I'll will them to you and no other.

You already know that this took place in 1860. The year before, about the month of August, at the age of forty-two, I had become a theologian--that is, I copied the theological studies of a priest at Nictheroy, an old college-chum, who thus tactfully gave me my board and lodging. In that same month of August, 1859, he received a letter from the vicar of a small town in the interior, asking if he knew of an intelligent, discreet and patient person who would be willing, in return for generous wages, to serve as attendant to the invalid Colonel Felisbert. The priest proposed that I take the place, and I accepted it eagerly, for I was tired of copying Latin quotations and ecclesiastic formulas. First I went to Rio de Janeiro to take leave of a brother who lived at the capital, and from there I departed for the little village of the interior.

When I arrived there I heard bad news concerning the colonel. He was pictured to me as a disagreeable, harsh, exacting fellow; nobody could endure him, not even his own friends. He had used more attendants than medicines. In fact he had broken the faces of two of them. But to all this I replied that I had no fear of persons in good health, still less of invalids. So, after first visiting the vicar, who confirmed all that I had heard and recommended to me charity and forbearance, I turned toward the colonel's residence.

I found him on the veranda of his house, stretched out on a chair and suffering greatly. He received me fairly well. At first he examined me silently, piercing me with his two feline eyes; then a kind of malicious smile spread over his features, which were rather hard. Finally he declared to me that all the attendants he had ever engaged in his service hadn't been worth a button, that they slept too much, were impudent and spent their time courting the servants; two of them were even thieves.

"And you, are you a thief?"

"No, sir."

Then he asked me my name. Scarcely had I uttered it when he made a gesture of astonishment.

"Your name is Colombo?"

"No, sir. My name is Procopio Jose Gomes Vallongo."

Vallongo?--He came to the conclusion that this was no Christian name and proposed thenceforth to call me simply Procopio. I replied that it should be just as he pleased.

If I recall this incident, it is not only because it seems to me to give a good picture of the colonel, but also to show you that my reply made a very good impression upon him. The next day he told the vicar so, adding that he had never had a more sympathetic attendant. The fact is, we lived a regular honeymoon that lasted one week.

From the dawn of the eighth day I knew the life of my predecessors--a dog's life. I no longer slept. I no longer thought of anything, I was showered with insults and laughed at them from time to time with an air of resignation and submission, for I had discovered that this was a way of pleasing him. His impertinences proceeded as much from his malady as from his temperament. His illness was of the most complicated: he suffered from aneurism, rheumatism and three or four minor affections. He was nearly sixty, and since he had been five years old had been accustomed to having everybody at his beck and call. That he was surly one could well forgive; but he was also very malicious. He took pleasure in the grief and the humiliation of others. At the end of three months I was tired of putting up with him and had resolved to leave; only the opportunity was lacking.

But that came soon enough. One day, when I was a bit late in giving him a massage, he took his cane and struck me with it two or three times. That was the last straw. I told him on the spot that I was through with him and I went to pack my trunk. He came later to my room; he begged me to remain, assured me that there wasn't anything to be angry at, that I must excuse the ill-humoredness of old age ... He insisted so much that I agreed to stay.

"I am nearing the end, Procopio," he said to me that evening. "I can't live much longer. I am upon the verge of the grave. You will go to my burial, Procopio. Under no circumstances will I excuse you. You shall go, you shall pray over my tomb. And if you don't," he added, laughing, "my ghost will come at night and pull you by the legs. Do you believe in souls of the other world, Procopio?"

"Nonsense!"

"And why don't you, you blockhead?" he replied passionately, with distended eyes.

That is how he was in his peaceful intervals; what he was during his attacks of anger, you may well imagine!

He hit me no more with his cane, but his insults were the same, if not worse. With time I became hardened, I no longer heeded anything; I was an ignoramus, a camel, a bumpkin, an idiot, a loggerhead--I was everything! It must further be understood that I alone was favored with these pretty names. He had no relatives; there had been a nephew, but he had died of consumption. As to friends, those who came now and then to flatter him and indulge his whims made him but a short visit, five or ten minutes at the most. I alone was always present to receive his dictionary of insults. More than once I resolved to leave him; but as the vicar would exhort me not to abandon the colonel I always yielded in the end.

Not only were our relations becoming very much strained, but I was in a hurry to get back to Rio de Janeiro. At forty-two years of age one does not easily accustom himself to perpetual seclusion with a brutal, snarling old invalid, in the depths of a remote village. Just to give you an idea of my isolation, let it suffice to inform you that I didn't even read the newspapers; outside of some more or less important piece of news that was brought to the colonel, I knew nothing of what was doing in the world. I therefore yearned to get back to Rio at the first opportunity, even at the cost of breaking with the vicar. And I may as well add--since I am here making a general confession--that having spent nothing of my wages, I was itching to dissipate them at the capital.

Very probably my chance was approaching. The colonel was rapidly getting worse. He made his will, the notary receiving almost as many insults as did I. The invalid's treatment became more strict; short intervals of peace and rest became rarer than ever for me. Already I had lost the meagre measure of pity that made me forget the old invalid's excesses; within me there seethed a cauldron of aversion and hatred. At the beginning of the month of August I decided definitely to leave. The vicar and the doctor, finally accepting my explanations, asked me but a few days' more service. I gave them a month. At the end of that time I would depart, whatever might be the condition of the invalid. The vicar promised to find a substitute for me.

You'll see now what happened. On the evening of the 24th of August the colonel had a violent attack of anger; he struck me, he called me the vilest names, he threatened to shoot me; finally he threw in my face a plate of porridge that was too cold for him. The plate struck the wall and broke into a thousand fragments.

"You'll pay me for it, you thief!" he bellowed.

For a long time he grumbled. Towards eleven o'clock he gradually fell asleep. While he slept I took a book out of my pocket, a translation of an old d'Arlincourt romance which I had found lying about, and began to read it in his room, at a small distance from his bed. I was to wake him at midnight to give him his medicine; but, whether it was due to fatigue or to the influence of the book, I, too, before reaching the second page, fell asleep. The cries of the colonel awoke me with a start; in an instant I was up. He, apparently in a delirium, continued to utter the same cries; finally he seized his water-bottle and threw it at my face. I could not get out of the way in time; the bottle hit me in the left cheek, and the pain was so acute that I almost lost consciousness. With a leap I rushed upon the invalid; I tightened my hands around his neck; he struggled several moments; I strangled him.

When I beheld that he no longer breathed, I stepped back in terror. I cried out; but nobody heard me. Then, approaching the bed once more, I shook him so as to bring him back to life. It was too late; the aneurism had burst, and the colonel was dead. I went into the adjoining room, and for two hours I did not dare to return. It is impossible for me to express all that I felt during that time. It was intense stupefaction, a kind of vague and vacant delirium. It seemed to me that I saw faces grinning on the walls; I heard muffled voices. The cries of the victim, the cries uttered before the struggle and during its wild moments continued to reverberate within me, and the air, in whatever direction I turned, seemed to shake with convulsions. Do not imagine that I am inventing pictures or aiming at verbal style. I swear to you that I heard distinctly voices that were crying at me: "Murderer; Murderer!"

All was quiet in the house. The tick-tick of the clock, very even, slow, dryly metrical, increased the silence and solitude. I put my ear to the door of the room, in hope of hearing a groan, a word, an insult, anything that would be a sign of life, that might bring back peace to my conscience; I was ready to let myself be struck ten, twenty, a hundred times, by the colonel's hand. But, nothing--all was silent. I began to pace the room aimlessly; I sat down, I brought my hands despairingly to my head; I repented ever having come to the place.

"Cursed be the hour in which I ever accepted such a position," I cried. And I flamed with resentment against the priest of Nichteroy, against the doctor, the vicar--against all those who had procured the place for me and forced me to remain there so long. They, too, I convinced myself, were accomplices in my crime.

As the silence finally terrified me, I opened a window, in the hope of hearing at least the murmuring of the wind. But no wind was blowing. The night was peaceful. The stars were sparkling with the indifference of those who remove their hats before a passing funeral procession and continue to speak of other things. I remained at the window for some time, my elbows on the sill, my gaze seeking to penetrate the night, forcing myself to make a mental summary of my life so that

I might escape the present agony. I believe it was only then that I thought clearly about the penalty of my crime. I saw myself already being accused and threatened with dire punishment. From this moment fear complicated my feeling of remorse. I felt my hair stand on end. A few minutes later I saw three or four human shapes spying at me from the terrace, where they seemed to be waiting in ambush; I withdrew; the shapes vanished into the air; it had been an hallucination.

Before daybreak I bandaged the wounds that I had received in the face. Then only did I pluck up enough courage to return to the other room. Twice I started, only to turn back; but it must be done, so I entered. Even then, I did not at first go to the bed. My legs shook, my heart pounded. I thought of flight; but that would have been a confession of the crime.... It was on the contrary very important for me to hide all traces of it. I approached the bed. I looked at the corpse, with its widely distended eyes and its mouth gaping, as if uttering the eternal reproach of the centuries: "Cain, what hast thou done with thy brother?" I discovered on the neck the marks of my nails; I buttoned the shirt to the top, and threw the bed-cover up to the dead man's chin. Then I called a servant and told him that the colonel had died towards morning; I sent him to notify the vicar and the doctor.

The first idea that came to me was to leave as soon as possible under the pretext that my brother was ill; and in reality I had received, several days before, from Rio, a letter telling me that he was not at all well. But I considered that my immediate departure might arouse suspicion, and I decided to wait. I laid out the corpse myself, with the assistance of an old, near-sighted negro. I remained continually in the room of the dead. I trembled lest something out of the way should be discovered. I wanted to assure myself that no mistrust could be read upon the faces of the others; but I did not dare to look any person in the eye. Everything made me impatient; the going and coming of those who, on tip-toe crossed the room; their whisperings; the ceremonies and the prayers of the vicar.... The hour having come, I closed the coffin, but with trembling hands, so trembling that somebody noticed it and commented upon it aloud, with pity.

"Poor Procopio! Despite what he has suffered from his master, he is strongly moved."

It sounded like irony to me. I was anxious to have it all over with. We went out. Once in the street the passing from semi-obscurity to daylight dazed me and

I staggered. I began to fear that it would no longer be possible for me to conceal the crime. I kept my eyes steadily fixed upon the ground and took my place in the procession. When all was over, I breathed once more. I was at peace with man. But I was not at peace with my conscience, and the first nights, naturally, I spent in restlessness and affliction. Need I tell you that I hastened to return to Rio de Janeiro, and that I dwelt there in terror and suspense, although far removed from the scene of the crime? I never smiled; I scarcely spoke; I ate very little; I suffered hallucinations and nightmares....

"Let the dead rest in peace," they would say to me. "It is out of all reason to show so much melancholy."

And I was happy to find how people interpreted my symptoms, and praised the dead man highly, calling him a good soul, surly, in truth, but with a heart of gold. And as I spoke in such wise, I convinced myself, at least for a few moments at a time. Another interesting phenomenon was taking place within me--I tell it to you because you will perhaps make some useful deduction from it--and that was, although I had very little religion in me, I had a mass sung for the eternal rest of the colonel at the Church of the Blessed Sacrament. I sent out no invitations to it, I did not whisper a word of it to anybody; I went there alone. I knelt during the whole service and made many signs of the cross. I paid the priest double and distributed alms at the door, all in the name of the deceased.

I wished to deceive nobody. The proof of this lies in the fact that I did all this without letting any other know. To complete this incident, I may add that I never mentioned the colonel without repeating, "May his soul rest in peace!" And I told several funny anecdotes about him, some amusing caprices of his ...

About a week after my arrival at Rio I received a letter from the vicar. He announced that the will of the colonel had been opened and that I was there designated as his sole heir. Imagine my stupefaction! I was sure that I had read wrongly; I showed it to my brother, to friends; they all read the same thing. It was there in black and white, I was really the sole heir of the colonel. Then I suddenly thought that this was a trap to catch me, but then I considered that there were other ways of arresting me, if the crime had been discovered. Moreover, I knew the vicar's honesty, and I was sure that he would not be a party to such a plan. I reread the letter five times, ten times, a hundred times; it was true. I was the colonel's sole heir!

"How much was he worth?" my brother asked me.

"I don't know, but I know that he was very wealthy."

"Really, he's shown that he was a very true friend to you."

"He certainly was--he was...."

Thus, by a strange irony of fate, all the colonel's wealth came into my hands. At first I thought of refusing the legacy. It seemed odious to take a sou of that inheritance; it seemed worse than the reward of a hired assassin. For three days this thought obsessed me; but more and more I was thrust against this consideration: that my refusal would not fail to awake suspicion. Finally I settled upon a compromise; I would accept the inheritance and would distribute it in small sums, secretly.

This was not merely scruple on my part, it was also the desire to redeem my crime by virtuous deeds; and it seemed the only way to recover my peace of mind and feel that accounts were straight.

I made hurried preparations and left. As I neared the little village the sad event returned obstinately to my memory. Everything about the place, as I looked at it once again, suggested tragic deeds. At every turn in the road I seemed to see the ghost of the colonel loom. And despite myself, I evoked in my imagination his cries, his struggles, his looks on that horrible night of the crime....

Crime or struggle? Really, it was rather a struggle; I had been attacked, I had defended myself; and in self-defence.... It had been an unfortunate struggle, a genuine tragedy. This idea gripped me. And I reviewed all the abuse he had heaped upon me; I counted the blows, the names ... It was not the colonel's fault, that I knew well; it was his affliction that made him so peevish and even wicked. But I pardoned all, everything!... The worst of it was the end of that fatal night ... I also considered that in any case the colonel had not long to live. His days were numbered; did not he himself feel that? Didn't he say every now and then, "How much longer have I to live? Two weeks, or one, perhaps less?"

This was not life, it was slow agony, if one may so name the continual martyrdom of that poor man.... And who knows, who can say that the struggle and his death were not simply a coincidence? That was after all quite possible, it was even most probable; careful weighing of the matter showed that it couldn't have been otherwise. At length this idea, too, engraved itself upon my mind....

Something tugged at my heart as I entered the village; I wanted to run back;

but I dominated my emotions and I pressed forward. I was received with a shower of congratulations. The vicar communicated to me the particulars of the will, enumerated the pious gifts, and, as he spoke, praised the Christian forbearance and the faithfulness which I had shown in my care of the deceased, who, despite his temper and brutality, had so well demonstrated his gratitude.

"Certainly," I said, looking nervously around.

I was astounded. Everybody praised my conduct. Such patience, such devotion. The first formalities of the inventory detained me for a while; I chose a solicitor; things followed their course in regular fashion. During this time there was much talk of the colonel. People came and told me tales about him, but without observing the priest's moderation. I defended the memory of the colonel. I recalled his good qualities, his virtues; had he not been austere?...

"Austere!" they would interrupt. "Nonsense! He is dead, and it's all over now. But he was a regular demon!"

And they would cite incidents and relate the colonel's perversities, some of which were nothing less than extraordinary.

Need I confess it? At first I listened to all this talk with great curiosity; then, a queer pleasure penetrated my heart, a pleasure from which, sincerely, I tried to escape. And I continued to defend the colonel; I explained him, I attributed much of the fault-finding to local animosity; I admitted, yes, I admitted that he had been a trifle exacting, somewhat violent....

"Somewhat! Why he was as furious as a snake!" exclaimed the barber.

And all--the collector, the apothecary, the clerk--all were of the same opinion. And they would start to relate other anecdotes. They reviewed the entire life of the deceased. The old folks took particular delight in recalling the cruelties of his youth. And that queer pleasure, intimate, mute, insidious, grew within me--a sort of moral tape-worm whose coils I tore out in vain, for they would immediately form again and take firmer hold than ever.

The formalities of the inventory afforded me a little relief; moreover, public opinion was so unanimously unfavorable to the colonel that little by little the place lost the lugubrious aspect that had at first struck me. At last I entered into possession of the legacy, which I converted into land-titles and cash.

Several months had elapsed, and the idea of distributing the inheritance in charity and pious donations was by no means so strong as it had at first been; it even seemed to me that this would be sheer affectation. I revised my initial plan; I gave away several insignificant sums to the poor; I presented the village church with a few new ornaments; I gave several thousand francs to the Sacred House of Mercy, etc. I did not forget to erect a monument upon the colonel's grave--a very simple monument, all marble, the work of a Neapolitan sculptor who remained at Rio until 1866, and who has since died, I believe, in Paraguay.

Years have gone by. My memory has become vague and unreliable. Sometimes I think of the colonel, but without feeling again the terrors of those early days. All the doctors to whom I have described his afflictions have been unanimous as regards the inevitable end in store for the invalid, and were indeed surprised that he should so long have resisted. It is just possible that I may have involuntarily exaggerated the description of his various symptoms; but the truth is that he was sure of sudden death, even had this fatality not occurred....

Good-bye, my dear sir. If you deem these notes not totally devoid of value reward me for them with a marble tomb, and place there for my epitaph this variant which I have made of the divine sermon on the mount:

"Blessed are they who possess, for they shall be consoled."

THE FORTUNE-TELLER
By Joaquim Maria Machado de Assis

Hamlet observes to Horatio that there are more things in heaven and earth than are dreamt of in our philosophy. This was the selfsame explanation that was given by beautiful Rita to her lover, Camillo, on a certain Friday of November, 1869, when Camillo laughed at her for having gone, the previous evening, to consult a fortune-teller. The only difference is that she made her explanation in other words.

"Laugh, laugh. That's just like you men; you don't believe in anything. Well, let me tell you, I went there and she guessed the reason for my coming before I ever spoke a word. Scarcely had she begun to lay out the cards when she said to me: 'The lady likes a certain person ...' I confessed that it was so, and then she continued to rearrange the cards in various combinations, finally telling me that I was afraid you would forget me, but that there were no grounds for my fear."

"She was wrong!" interrupted Camillo with a laugh.

"Don't say that, Camillo. If you only realized in what anguish I went there, all on account of you. You know. I've told you before. Don't laugh at me; don't poke fun at me...."

Camillo seized her hands and gazed into her eyes earnestly and long. He swore that he loved her ever so much, that her fears were childish; in any case, should she ever harbor a fear, the best fortune-teller to consult was he himself. Then he reproved her, saying that it was imprudent to visit such houses. Villela might learn of it, and then ...

"Impossible! I was exceedingly careful when I entered the place."

"Where is the house?"

"Near here. On Guarda-Velha Street. Nobody was passing by at the time. Rest easy. I'm not a fool."

Camillo laughed again.

"Do you really believe in such things?" he asked.

It was at this point that she translated Hamlet into every-day speech, assuring her lover that there was many a true, mysterious thing in this world. If he was skeptical, let him have patience. One thing, however, was certain: the card reader had guessed everything. What more could he desire? The best proof was that at this moment she was at ease and content.

He was about to speak, but he restrained himself. He did not wish to destroy her illusions. He, too, when a child, and even later, had been superstitious, filled with an arsenal of beliefs which his mother had instilled, and which had disappeared by the time he reached twenty. The day on which he rid himself of all this parasitic vegetation, leaving behind only the trunk of religion, he wrapped his superstition and his religion (which had both been inculcated by his mother) in the same doubt, and soon arrived at a single, total negation. Camillo believed in nothing. Why? He could not have answered; he had not a solitary reason; he was content simply to deny everything. But I express myself ill, for to deny is in a sense to affirm, and he did not formulate his unbelief. Before the great mystery he simply shrugged his shoulders and went on.

The lovers parted in good spirits, he more happy than she. Rita was sure that she was loved; but Camillo was not only sure that she loved him, but saw how she trembled for him and even took risks, running to fortune-tellers. However much he had reproved her for this, he could not help feeling flattered by it. Their secret meeting-place was in the old Barbonos street at the home of a woman that came from Rita's province. Rita went off through Mangueiras street, in the direction of Botafogo, where she resided; Camillo entered Guarda-Velha street, keeping his eye open, as he passed, for the home of the card reader.

Villela, Camillo and Rita: three names, one adventure and no explanation of how it all began. Let us proceed to explain. The first two were friends since earliest childhood. Villela had entered the magistracy. Camillo found employment with the government, against the will of his father, who desired him to embrace the medical profession. But his father had died, and Camillo preferred to be nothing at all, until his mother had procured him a departmental position. At the beginning of the year

1869 Villela returned from the interior, where he had married a silly beauty; he abandoned the magistracy and came hither to open a lawyer's office. Camillo had secured a house for him near Botafogo and had welcomed him home.

"Is this the gentleman?" exclaimed Rita, offering Camillo her hand. "You can't imagine how highly my husband thinks of you. He was always talking about you."

Camillo and Villela looked at each other tenderly. They were true friends. Afterwards, Camillo confessed to himself that Villela's wife did not at all belie the enthusiastic letters her husband had written to him. Really, she was most prepossessing, lively in her movements, her eyes burning, her mouth plastic and piquantly inquiring. Rita was a trifle older than both the men: she was thirty, Villela twenty-nine and Camillo twenty-six. The grave bearing of Villela gave him the appearance of being much older than his wife, while Camillo was but a child in moral and practical life.... He possessed neither experience nor intuition.

The three became closely bound. Propinquity bred intimacy. Shortly afterwards Camillo's mother died, and in this catastrophe, for such it was, the other two showed themselves to be genuine friends of his. Villela took charge of the interment, of the church services and the settlement of the affairs of the deceased; Rita dispensed consolation, and none could do it better.

Just how this intimacy between Camillo and Rita grew to love he never knew. The truth is that he enjoyed passing the hours at her side; she was his spiritual nurse, almost a sister,--but most of all she was a woman, and beautiful. The aroma of femininity: this is what he yearned for in her, and about her, seeking to incorporate it into himself. They read the same books, they went together to the theatre or for walks. He taught her cards and chess, and they played of nights;--she badly,--he, to make himself agreeable, but little less badly. Thus much, as far as external things are concerned. And now came personal intimacies, the timorous eyes of Rita, that so often sought his own, consulting them before they questioned those of her own husband,--the touches of cold hands, and unwonted communion. On one of his birthdays he received from Villela a costly cane, and from Rita, a hastily pencilled, ordinary note expressing good wishes. It was then that he learned to read within his own heart; he could not tear his eyes away from the missive. Commonplace words, it is true; but there are sublime commonplaces,--or at least, delightful ones. The old chaise in which for the first time you rode with your beloved, snuggled together, is as good as the chariot of Apollo. Such is man, and such are the circumstances that surround him.

Camillo sincerely wished to flee the situation, but it was already beyond his power. Rita, like a serpent, was charming him, winding her coils about him; she was crushing his bones, darting her venomous fangs into his lips. He was helpless, overcome. Vexation, fear, remorse, desire,--all this he felt, in a strange confusion. But the battle was short and the victory deliriously intoxicating. Farewell, all scruple! The shoe now fitted snugly enough upon the foot, and there they were both, launched upon the high road, arm in arm, joyfully treading the grass and the gravel, without suffering anything more than lonesomeness when they were away from each other. As to Villela, his confidence in his wife and his esteem for his friend continued the same as before.

One day, however, Camillo received an anonymous letter, which called him immoral and perfidious, and warned him that his adventure was known to all. Camillo took fright, and, in order to ward off suspicion, began to make his visits to Villela's house more rare. The latter asked him the reason for his prolonged absence. Camillo answered that the cause was a youthful flirtation. Simplicity evolved into cunning. Camillo's absences became longer and longer, and then his visits ceased entirely. Into this course there may have entered a little self-respect,--the idea of diminishing his obligations to the husband in order to make his own actions appear less treacherous.

It was at this juncture that Rita, uncertain and in fear, ran to the fortune-teller to consult her upon the real reason for Camillo's actions. As we have seen, the card reader restored the wife's confidence and the young man reproved her for having done what she did. A few weeks passed. Camillo received two or three more anonymous letters, written with such passionate anger that they could not have been prompted by mere regard for virtue; surely they came from some violent rival of his. In this opinion Rita concurred, formulating, in ill-composed words of her own, this thought: virtue is indolent and niggardly, wasting neither time nor paper; only self-interest is alert and prodigal.

But this did not help to ease Camillo; he now feared lest the anonymous writer should inform Villela, in which case the catastrophe would follow fast and implacably. Rita agreed that this was possible.

"Very well," she said. "Give me the envelopes in which the letters came, so that I may compare the handwriting with that of the mail which comes to him. If any arrives with writing resembling the anonymous script, I'll keep it and tear it up ..."

But no such letter appeared. A short time after this, however, Villela commenced to grow grave, speaking very little, as if something weighed upon his mind. Rita hurried to communicate the change to her lover, and they discussed the matter earnestly. Her opinion was that Camillo should renew his visits to their home, and sound her husband; it might be that Villela would confide to him some business worry. With this Camillo disagreed; to appear after so many months was to confirm the suspicions and denunciations of the anonymous letters. It was better to be very careful, to give each other up for several weeks. They arranged means for communicating with each other in case of necessity and separated, in tears.

On the following day Camillo received at his department this letter from Villela: "Come immediately to our house; I must talk to you without delay." It was past noon. Camillo left at once; as he reached the street it occurred to him that it would have been much more natural for Villela to have called him to his office; why to his house? All this betokened a very urgent matter; moreover, whether it was reality or illusion, it seemed to Camillo that the letter was written in a trembling hand. He sought to establish a connection between all these things and the news Rita had brought him the night before.

"Come immediately to our house; I must talk to you without delay," he repeated, his eyes staring at the note.

In his mind's eye he beheld the climax of a drama,--Rita cowed, weeping; Villela indignant, seizing his pen and dashing off the letter, certain that he, Camillo, would answer in person, and waiting to kill him as he entered. Camillo shuddered with terror; then he smiled weakly; in any event the idea of drawing back was repugnant to him. So he continued on his way. As he walked it occurred to him to step into his rooms; he might find there a message from Rita explaining everything. But he found nothing, nobody. He returned to the street, and the thought that they had been discovered grew every moment more convincing; yes, the author of the previous anonymous communications must have denounced him to the husband; perhaps by now Villela knew all. The very suspension of his calls without any apparent reason, with the flimsiest of pretexts, would confirm everything else.

Camillo walked hastily along, agitated, nervous. He did not read the letter again, but the words hovered persistently before his eyes; or else,--which was even worse--they seemed to be murmured into his ears by the voice of Villela himself. "Come immediately to our house; I must talk to you without delay." Spoken thus by the voice of the other they seemed pregnant with mystery and menace. Come immediately,--why? It was now nearly one o'clock. Camillo's agitation waxed greater with each passing moment. So clearly did he imagine what was about to take place that he began to believe it a reality, to see it before his very eyes. Yes, without a doubt, he was afraid. He even considered arming himself, thinking that if nothing should happen he would lose nothing by this useful precaution. But at once he rejected the idea, angry with himself, and hastened his step towards Carioca square, there to take a tilbury. He arrived, entered and ordered the driver to be off at full speed.

"The sooner the better," he thought. "I can't stand this uncertainty."

But the very sound of the horse's clattering hoofs increased his agitation. Time was flying, and he would be face to face with danger soon enough. When they had come almost to the end of Guarda-Velha street the tilbury had to come to a stop; the thoroughfare was blocked by a coach that had broken down. Camillo surveyed the obstruction and decided to wait. After five minutes had gone by, he noticed that there at his left, at the very foot of the tilbury, was the fortune teller's house,--the very same as Rita had once consulted. Never, as at this moment, had he so desired to believe in card-reading. He looked closer, saw that the windows were closed, while all the others on the street were opened, filled with folks curious to see what was the matter. It looked for all the world like the dwelling of indifferent Fate.

Camillo leaned back in his seat so as to shut all this from view. His excitement was intense, extraordinary, and from the deep, hidden recesses of his mind there began to emerge spectres of early childhood, old beliefs, banished superstitions. The coachman proposed another route; he shook his head and said that he would wait. He leaned forward to get a better look at the card-reader's house ... Then he made a gesture of self-ridicule: it had entered his mind to consult the fortune-teller, who seemed to be hovering over him, far, far above, with vast, ash-colored wings; she disappeared, reappeared, and then her image was lost; then, in a few moments, the ash-colored wings stirred again, nearer, flying about him in narrowing circles ... In the street men were shouting, dragging away the coach.

"There! Now! Push! That's it! Now!"

In a short while the obstruction was removed. Camillo closed his eyes, trying to think of other things; but the voice of Rita's husband whispered into his ears the words of the letter: "Come immediately ..." And he could behold the anguish of the drama. He trembled. The house seemed to look right at him. His feet instinctively moved as if to leave the carriage and go in ... Camillo found himself before a long, opaque veil ... he thought rapidly of the inexplicability of so many things. The voice of his mother was repeating to him a host of extraordinary happenings; and the very sentence of the Prince of Denmark kept echoing within him:

"There are more things in heaven and earth, Horatio,   Than are dreamt of in our philosophy."

What could he lose by it, if...?

He jumped out to the pavement, just before the fortune-teller's door; he told the driver to wait for him, and hastened into the entry, ascending the stairs. There was little light, the stairs were worn away from the many feet that had sought them, the banister was smooth and sticky; but he saw and felt nothing. He stumbled up the stairs and knocked. Nobody appearing, he was about to go down; but it was too late now,--curiosity was whipping his blood and his heart beat with violent throbs; he turned back to the door, and knocked once, twice, three times. He beheld a woman; it was the card-reader. Camillo said that he had come to consult her, and she bade him enter. Thence they climbed to the attic by a staircase even worse than the first and buried in deeper gloom. At the top there was a garret, ill lighted by a small window. Old furniture, somber walls, and an air of poverty augmented, rather than destroyed, the prestige of the occupant.

The fortune-teller told him to be seated before the table, and she sat down on the opposite side with her back to the window, so that whatever little light came from without fell full upon Camillo's face. She opened a drawer and took out a pack of worn, filthy cards. While she rapidly shuffled them she peered at him closely, not so much with a direct gaze as from under her eyes. She was a woman of forty, Italian, thin and swarthy, with large, sharp, cunning eyes. She placed three cards upon the table, and said:

"Let us first see what has brought you here. The gentleman has just received a severe shock and is in great fear ..."

Camillo, astonished, nodded affirmatively.

"And he wishes to know," she continued, "whether anything will happen to him or not ..."

"To me and to her," he explained, excitedly.

The fortune-teller did not smile; she simply told him to wait. She took the cards hastily once more and shuffled them with her long tapering fingers whose nails were so long and unclean from neglect; she shuffled them well, once, twice, thrice; then she began to lay them out. Camillo's eyes were riveted upon her in anxious curiosity.

"The cards tell me ..."

Camillo leaned forward to drink in her words one by one. Then she told him to fear nothing. Nothing would happen to him or to the other. He, the third, was aware of nought. Nevertheless, great caution was indispensable; envy and rivalry were at work. She spoke to him of the love that bound them, of Rita's beauty ... Camillo was bewildered. The fortune-teller stopped talking, gathered the cards and locked them in the drawer.

"The lady has restored peace to my spirit," he said, offering her his hand across the table and pressing that of the card-reader.

She arose, laughing.

"Go," she said. "Go, *ragazzo innamorato* ..."[4]

And arising, she touched his head with her index finger. Camillo shuddered, as if it were the hand of one of the original sybils, and he, too, arose. The fortune-teller went to the bureau, upon which lay a plate of raisins, took a cluster of them and commenced to eat them, showing two rows of teeth that were as white as her nails were black. Even in this common action the woman possessed an air all her own. Camillo, anxious to leave, was at a loss how much to pay; he did not know her fee.

"Raisins cost money," he said, at length, taking out his pocket-book. "How much do you want to send for?"

"Ask your heart," she replied.

---

4   Italian for "love-sick boy,"
"young lover," etc.

Camillo took out a note for ten milreis'[5] and gave it to her. The eyes of the card-reader sparkled. Her usual fee was two milreis.

"I can see easily that the gentleman loves his lady very much ... And well he may. For she loves the gentleman very deeply, too. Go, go in peace, with your mind at ease. And take care as you descend the staircase,--it's dark. Don't forget your hat ..."

The fortune-teller had already placed the note in her pocket, and accompanied him down the stairs, chatting rather gaily. At the bottom of the first flight Camillo bid her good-bye and ran down the stairs that led to the street, while the card-reader, rejoicing in her large fee, turned back to the garret, humming a barcarolle. Camillo found the tilbury waiting for him; the street was now clear. He entered and the driver whipped his horse into a fast trot.

To Camillo everything had now changed for the better and his affairs assumed a brighter aspect; the sky was clear and the faces of the people he passed were all so merry. He even began to laugh at his fears, which he now saw were puerile; he re-called the language of Villela's letter and perceived at once that it was most friendly and familiar. How in the world had he ever been able to read any threat of danger into those words! He suddenly realized that they were urgent, however, and that he had done ill to delay so long; it might be some very serious business affair.

"Faster, faster!" he cried to the driver.

And he began to think of a plausible explanation of his delay; he even con-templated taking advantage of this incident to re-establish his former intimacy in Villela's household ... Together with his plans there kept echoing in his soul the words of the fortune-teller. In truth, she had guessed the object of his visit, his own state of mind, and the existence of a third; why, then, wasn't it reasonable to suppose that she had guessed the rest correctly, too? For, the unknown present is the same as the future. And thus, slowly and persistently the young man's child-hood superstitions attained the upper hand and mystery clutched him in its iron claws. At times he was ready to burst into laughter, and with a certain vexation he did laugh at himself. But the woman, the cards, her dry, reassuring words, and her good-bye--"Go, go, *ragazzo innamorato*," and finally, that farewell barcarolle, so lively and gracious,--such were the new elements which, together with the old,

5   In United States money ten Brazilian milreis are equivalent   to about $5.50.

formed within him a new and abiding faith.

The truth is that his heart was happy and impatient, recalling the happy hours of the past and anticipating those yet to come. As he passed through Gloria street Camillo gazed across the sea, far across where the waters and the heaven meet in endless embrace, and the sight gave him a sensation of the future,--long, long and infinite.

From here it was but a moment's drive to Villela's home. He stepped out, thrust the iron garden gate open and entered. The house was silent. He ran up the six stone steps and scarcely had he had time to knock when the door opened and Villela loomed before him.

"Pardon my delay. It was impossible to come sooner. What is the matter?"

Villela made no reply. His features were distorted; he beckoned Camillo to step within. As he entered, Camillo could not repress a cry of horror:--there upon the sofa lay Rita, dead in a pool of blood. Villela seized the lover by the throat and, with two bullets, stretched him dead upon the floor.

LIFE
By Joaquim Maria Machado de Assis

End of time. Ahasverus, seated upon a rock, gazes for a long while upon the horizon, athwart which wing two eagles, crossing each other in their path. He meditates, then falls into a doze. The day wanes.

AHASVERUS. I have come to the end of time; this is the threshold of eternity. The earth is deserted; no other man breathes the air of life. I am the last; I can die. Die! Precious thought! For centuries of centuries I have lived, wearied, mortified, wandering ever, but now the centuries are coming to an end, and I shall die with them. Ancient nature, farewell! Azure sky, clouds ever reborn, roses of a day and of every day, perennial waters, hostile earth that never would devour my bones, farewell! The eternal wanderer will wander no longer. God may pardon me if He wishes, but death will console me. That mountain is as unyielding as my grief; those eagles that fly yonder must be as famished as my despair. Shall you, too, die, divine eagles?

PROMETHEUS. Of a surety the race of man is perished; the earth is bare of them.

AHASVERUS. I hear a voice.... The voice of a human being? Implacable heavens, am I not then the last? He approaches.... Who are you? There shines in your large eyes something like the mysterious light of the archangels of Israel; you are not a human being?...

PROMETHEUS. No.

AHASVERUS. Of a race divine, then?

PROMETHEUS. You have said it.

AHASVERUS. I do not know you; but what matters it that I do not? You are not a human being; then I may die; for I am the last and I close the gate of life.

PROMETHEUS. Life, like ancient Thebes, has a hundred gates. You close one, and others will open. You are the last of your species? Then another better species will come, made not of clay, but of the light itself. Yes, last of men, all the common spirits will perish forever; the flower of them it is which will return to earth and rule. The ages will be rectified. Evil will end; the winds will thenceforth scatter neither the germs of death nor the clamor of the oppressed, but only the song of love everlasting and the benediction of universal justice....

AHASVERUS. What can all this posthumous joy matter to the species that dies with me? Believe me, you who are immortal, to the bones that rot in the earth the purples of Sidonia are worthless. What you tell me is even better than what Campanella dreamed. In that man's ideal city there were delights and ills; yours excludes all mortal and physical ailments. May the Lord hear you! But let me go and die.

PROMETHEUS. Go, go. But why this haste to end your days?

AHASVERUS. The haste of a man who has lived for thousands of years. Yes, thousands of years. Men who existed scarcely scores of them invented a feeling of ennui, **tedium vitae**, which they could never know, at least in all its implacable and vast reality, because it is necessary to have journeyed through all the generations and all the cataclysms to feel that profound surfeit of existence.

PROMETHEUS. Thousands of years?

AHASVERUS. My name Is Ahasverus; I dwelt in Jerusalem at the time they were about to crucify Christ. When he passed my door he weakened under the burden of the beam that he carried on his shoulders, and I thrust him onward, admonishing him not to stop, not to rest, to continue on his way to the hill where he was to be crucified.... Then there came a voice from heaven, telling me that I, too, should have to journey forever, continuously, until the end of time. Such was my crime; I felt no pity for him who was going to his death. I do not know myself how it came about. The Pharisees said that the son of Mary had come to destroy the law, and that he must be slain; I, ignorant wretch, wished to display my zeal and hence my action of that day. How many times have I seen the same thing since, traveling unceasingly through cities and ages! Whenever zealotry penetrated into a submissive soul, it became cruel or ridiculous. My crime was unpardonable.

PROMETHEUS. A grave crime, in truth, but the punishment was lenient. The other men read but a chapter of life; you have read the whole book. What does one chapter know of the other chapter? Nothing. But he who has read them all, connects them and concludes. Are there melancholy pages? There are merry and happy ones, too. Tragic convulsion precedes that of laughter; life burgeons from death; swans and swallows change climate, without ever abandoning it entirely; and thus all is harmonized and begun anew. You have beheld this, not ten times, not a thousand times, but ever; you have beheld the magnificence of the earth curing the affliction of the soul, and the joy of the soul compensating for the desolation of things; the alternating dance of Nature, who gives her left hand to Job and her right to Sardanapalus.

AHASVERUS. What do you know of my life? Nothing; you are ignorant of human existence.

PROMETHEUS. I, ignorant of human life? How laughable! Come, perpetual man, explain yourself. Tell me everything; you left Jerusalem ...

AHASVERUS. I left Jerusalem. I began my wandering through the ages. I journeyed everywhere, whatever the race, the creed, the tongue; suns and snows, barbarous and civilized peoples, islands, continents; wherever a man breathed, there breathed I. I never labored. Labor is a refuge, and that refuge was denied me. Every morning I found upon me the necessary money for the day ... See; this is the last apportionment. Go, for I need you no longer. (*He draws forth the money and throws it away.*) I did not work; I just journeyed, ever and ever, one day after another, year after year unendingly, century after century. Eternal justice knew what it was doing: it added idleness to eternity. One generation bequeathed me to the other. The languages, as they died, preserved my name like a fossil. With the passing of time all was forgotten; the heroes faded into myths, into shadow, and history crumbled to fragments, only two or three vague, remote characteristics remaining to it. And I saw them in changing aspect. You spoke of a chapter? Happy are those who read only one chapter of life. Those who depart at the birth of empires bear with them the impression of their perpetuity; those who die at their fall, are buried in the hope of their restoration; but do you not realize what it is to see the same things unceasingly,--the same alternation of prosperity and desolation, desolation and prosperity, eternal obsequies and eternal halleluiahs, dawn upon dawn, sunset upon sunset?

PROMETHEUS. But you did not suffer, I believe. It is something not to suffer.

AHASVERUS. Yes, but I saw other men suffer, and in the end the spectacle of joy gave me the same sensations as the discourses of an idiot. Fatalities of flesh and blood, unending strife,--I saw all pass before my eyes, until night caused me to lose my taste for day, and now I cannot distinguish flowers from thistles. Everything is confused in my wearied retina.

PROMETHEUS. But nothing pained you personally; and what about me, from time immemorial suffering the wrath of the gods?

AHASVERUS. You?

PROMETHEUS. My name is Prometheus.

AHASVERUS. You! Prometheus!

PROMETHEUS. And what was my crime? Out of clay and water I made the first men, and afterwards, seized with compassion, I stole for them fire from the sky. Such was my crime. Jupiter, who then reigned over Olympus, condemned me to the most cruel of tortures. Come, climb this rock with me.

AHASVERUS. You are telling me a tale. I know that Hellenic myth.

PROMETHEUS. Incredulous old fellow! Come see the very chains that fettered me; it was an excessive penalty for no crime whatever; but divine pride is terrible ... See; there they are ...

AHASVERUS. And time, which gnaws all things, does not desire them, then?

PROMETHEUS. They were wrought by a divine hand. Vulcan forged them. Two emissaries from heaven came to secure me to the rock, and an eagle, like that which now is flying across the horizon, kept gnawing at my liver without ever consuming it. This lasted for time beyond my reckoning. No, no, you cannot imagine this torture ...

AHASVERUS. Are you not deceiving me? You, Prometheus? Was that not, then, a figment of the ancient imagination?

PROMETHEUS. Look well at me; touch these hands. See whether I really exist.

AHASVERUS. Then Moses lied to me. You are Prometheus, creator of the first men?

PROMETHEUS. That was my crime.

AHASVERUS. Yes, it was your crime,--an artifice of hell; your crime was inexpiable. You should have remained forever, bound and devoured,--you, the origin of the ills that afflict me. I lacked compassion, it is true; but you, who gave me life, perverse divinity, were the cause of all.

PROMETHEUS. Approaching death confuses your reason.

AHASVERUS. Yes, it is you; you have the Olympic forehead, strong and beautiful Titan; it is you indeed ... Are these your chains? I see upon them no trace of your tears.

PROMETHEUS. I wept them for your humankind.

AHASVERUS. And humanity wept far more because of your crime.

PROMETHEUS. Hear me, last of men, last of ingrates!

AHASVERUS. What need have I of your words? I desire your groans, perverse divinity. Here are the chains. See how I raise them; listen to the clank of the iron ... Who unbound you just now?

PROMETHEUS. Hercules.

AHASVERUS. Hercules ... See whether he will repeat his service now that you are to be bound anew.

PROMETHEUS. You are raving.

AHASVERUS. The sky gave you your first punishment, now earth will give you the second and the last. Not even Hercules will ever be able to break these fetters. See how I brandish them in the air, like feathers! for I represent the power of millennial despairs. All humanity is concentrated within me. Before I sink into the abyss, I will write upon this stone the epitaph of a world. I will summon the eagle, and it will come; I will tell it that the last man, on departing from life, leaves him a god as a gift.

PROMETHEUS. Poor, ignorant wretch, who rejects a throne! No, you cannot reject it.

AHASVERUS. Now it is you who are raving. Kneel, and let me manacle your arms. So, 'tis well you will resist no more. Bend this way; now your legs ...

PROMETHEUS. Have done, have done. It is the passions of earth turning upon me; but I, who am not a human being, do not know ingratitude. You will not be spared a jot of your destiny; it will be fulfilled to the letter. You yourself will be the new Hercules. I, who announced the glory of the other, now proclaim yours; and you will be no less generous than he.

AHASVERUS. Are you mad?

PROMETHEUS. The truth unknown to man is the madness of him who proclaims it. Proceed, and have done.

AHASVERUS. Glory pays nothing, and dies.

PROMETHEUS. This glory will never die. Have done; have done; show the sharp beak of the eagle where it is to devour my entrails. But hear me ... No, hear nothing; you cannot understand me.

AHASVERUS. Speak; speak.

PROMETHEUS. The ephemeral world cannot understand the world eternal; but you will be the link between the two.

AHASVERUS. Tell me everything.

PROMETHEUS. I speak nothing; fetter these wrists well, that I shall not flee,--so that I shall be here on your return. Tell you all? I have already told you that a new race shall people the earth, formed of the chosen spirits of the extinct humanity; the multitude of others will perish. A noble family, all-seeing and powerful, will be the perfect synthesis of the divine and the human. The times will be others, but between them and these a link is necessary, and you shall be that link.

AHASVERUS. I?

PROMETHEUS. You yourself; you, the chosen one; you, the King. Yes, Ahasverus. You shall be King. The Wanderer will find rest. The despised of men shall rule over mankind.

AHASVERUS. Wily Titan, you are deceiving me ... King,--I?

PROMETHEUS. You, King. Who else, then? The new world needs to be bound by a tradition, and none can speak of one to the other as you can. Thus there will be no gap between the two humanities. The perfect will proceed from the imperfect, and your lips will tell the new world its origin. You will relate to the new humanity all the ancient good and evil. And thus will you live anew like the tree whose dead branches are lopped off, only the flourishing ones being preserved, but here growth will be eternal.

AHASVERUS. Resplendent vision! I myself?

PROMETHEUS. Your very self.

AHASVERUS. These eyes ... these hands ... a new and better life ... Glorious vision! Titan, it is just. Just was the punishment; but equally just is the glorious remission of my sin. Shall I live? I myself? A new and better life? No, you are jesting with me.

PROMETHEUS. Very well, then; leave me. You will return some day, when this vast heaven will be open to let the spirits of the new life descend. You will find me here at peace. Go.

AHASVERUS. Shall I again greet the sun?

PROMETHEUS. The selfsame sun that is about to set. Friend sun, eye of time, nevermore shall your eyelids close. Gaze upon it, if you can.

AHASVERUS. I cannot.

PROMETHEUS. You will be able to, when the conditions of life shall have changed. Then your retina will gaze upon the sun without peril, for in the man of the future will be concentrated all that is best in nature, energizing or subtle, scintillating or pure.

AHASVERUS. Swear that you are not lying.

PROMETHEUS. You will see whether I lie.

AHASVERUS. Speak, speak on; tell me everything.

PROMETHEUS. The description of life is not worth the sensation of life; you shall experience it deeply. The bosom of Abraham in your old Scriptures is nothing but this final, perfect world. There you will greet David and the prophets. There will you tell to the astounded listeners, not only the great events of the extinct world, but also the ills they will never know: sickness, old age, grief, egotism, hypocrisy, abhorrent vanity, imbecility, and the rest. The soul, like the earth, will possess an incorruptible tunic.

AHASVERUS. I shall gaze ever on the immense blue sky?

PROMETHEUS. Behold how beautiful it is.

AHASVERUS. As beautiful and serene as eternal justice. Magnificent heaven, more beautiful than the tents of Caesar. I shall behold you forever; you will receive my thoughts, as before; you will grant me clear days, and friendly nights ...

PROMETHEUS. Dawn upon dawn.

AHASVERUS. Ah, speak on, speak on. Tell me everything. Let me unbind these chains ...

PROMETHEUS. Loosen them, new Hercules, last man of the old world, who shall be the first of the new. Such is your destiny; neither you nor I,--nobody can alter it. You go farther than your Moses. From the top of mount Nebo, at the point of death, he beheld the land of Jericho, which was to belong to his descendants and the Lord said unto him: "Thou hast seen with thine eyes, yet shalt not pass beyond." *You* shall pass beyond, Ahasverus; you shall dwell in Jericho.

AHASVERUS. Place your hand upon my head; look well at me; fill me with the reality of your prediction; let me breathe a little of the new, full life ... King, did you say?

PROMETHEUS. The chosen king of a chosen people.

AHASVERUS. It is not too much in recompense for the deep ignominy in which I have dwelt. Where one life heaped mire, another life will place a halo. Speak, speak on ... speak on ... (*He continues to dream. The two eagles draw near.*)

FIRST EAGLE. Ay, ay, ay! Alas for this last man; he is dying, yet he dreams of life.

SECOND EAGLE. Not so much that he hated it as that he loved it so much.

THE VENGEANCE OF FELIX
By Jose de Medeiros E Albuquerque (1867-)

Member of the Brazilian Academy of Letters

Old Felix had followed his trade of digger in all the quarries that Rio de Janeiro possessed. He was a sort of Hercules with huge limbs, but otherwise stupid as a post. His companions had nicknamed him Hardhead because of his obstinate character. Once an idea had penetrated his skull it would stick there like a gimlet and the devil himself couldn't pull it out. Because of this trait there arose quarrels, altercations on points of the smallest significance, which the man's acquaintances would purposely bring up, knowing his evil humor. But Felix, despite his vigorous and sanguine constitution, was by no means quick to anger, nor immediately responsive to injury; on the contrary he was exceedingly patient in his vindictiveness. For the longest time he would ruminate upon his vengeance, most astutely, and he would carry it out at the moment when he believed himself perfectly secure. Oh! His ruses were not of very great finesse and required very little talent; but by dint of considering and reconsidering the case, by dint of waiting patiently for the propitious opportunity to present itself, he finally would play some evil trick upon his comrades. So that nobody liked him.

Felix had married, but his wife did not long survive. Just long enough to leave him a son and a daughter, who grew up knowing little restraint, chumming around with all the good-for-nothings of the vicinity, plaguing all the neighbors, who on their part, were not slow to punish the rascals. Thus several years went by. The son became a notorious character, the daughter an impudent, cynical little runabout who, on certain occasions, would fill their rickety abode with her chatter about affairs concerning the "man" of so-and-so or such-and-such. And thus things were going when the old man took it into his head to fall ill. An excruciating rheumatism attacked both his legs, rendering him incapable of moving about, and confining him to an old, lame armchair that was balanced by a complicated arrangement of old boxes that could never be got to remain steady. The illness became chronic. The daughter helped out the finances of the house with her earnings as laundry-woman ... and perhaps by earnings of a different nature. Anyway, they got along. The old fellow, willy-nilly, spent his days invariably riveted to his armchair, groaning with pain at the least movement, swearing, fretting and fuming, despairing of life. And, since his daughter simply refused from the very beginning to let him have even a drop of brandy, he was perforce cured of his vice.

Just about this time there happened to them the worst of all possible adventures. The son, whom the father had not seen for several weeks, one fine day attacked a peaceful citizen and, with a terrible knife thrust in the stomach, despatched him to a better world; as to which event circumstances seemed so contrary that the son allowed himself to be arrested.

The old man was in the habit of reading his gazette religiously, from the first line to the last; thus he learned the news. And it was through the same newspaper that he followed the trial and learned of his son's conviction. This made him furious, not so much because of the sentence as because of a special circumstance. The policeman who had arrested his son was--just think of it!--Bernardo,--yes, Bernardo, his own neighbor--the same chap who would greet him daily with the ironic words: "How are things, Felix old boy? And when will you be ready for a waltz?"

Even on the day of imprisonment and during those that followed Bernardo had permitted himself these witty remarks.

Bernardo was a *cabra* of Bahai, a pretentious mulatto whose enormous head of hair, carefully parted in the middle into two flourishing masses, was kept so only through the services of odorous pomade that cost four sous a pot. He had been, in his day, a dishonest political henchman, well-known for his exploits; then, supported by the liberal leader whose election he had worked for, he escaped prison and entered the police service. At that time police officers were called "bats",--a sobriquet that troubled Bernardo very little. And it had been he--what anger flashed in old Felix's eyes as he thought of it!--he, whose past activities would well bear examination, he who had arrested Felix's son!...

From that moment one preoccupation alone filled Felix's hours--vengeance! This hatred dominated his existence and became the only power that could vanquish the ever-growing misery of his broken-down body. The mere thought that he could not grow well, while the *cabra* would daily continue to live in insolent impunity, was enough to give him convulsions of rage; he would foam at the mouth, gnash his teeth and, in that obtuse brain of his, concoct scheme upon scheme of vengeance, almost all of them impracticable, for he was chained to the spot in stupid impotence.

At times he would wish to call Bernardo and with thunderous violence pour torrents of insult upon his head. But what end would that serve? Felix's treacherous, cowardous nature counselled him to have prudence. So, on the first days after the arrest, when the mulatto would go by, the old man feigned slumber. Then, in the continuing uncertainty as to what method of vengeance to pursue, and in order not to let his hatred betray itself, he spoke to the policeman as if nothing had happened. Nevertheless there was one thing that puzzled him greatly: his daughter had said nothing to him about the entire affair. Did she know nothing about it? It was almost impossible that the mulatto, with his chatterbox habits, had not spoken of the matter. Had his daughter feared to shock him with the news? This was all the less probable since she had never had any particular love for him. Scarcely did a day pass that she did not call him a "good-for-nothing," "a lazy lout," and other similar tendernesses. So he breathed not a word, and continued to ruminate upon his vengeance.

Months rolled on. Far from getting better the illness increased. As soon as the old fellow tried to move, horrible pains seized him at every joint. His daughter maltreated him, and at the height of his attacks she would reply to his complaints that he'd do better if he left the house, and she even threatened to send him to the hospital. It was now June. The weather was one long succession of heavy rains; the invalid suffered atrociously from the cold and the damp, and his daughter, disgruntled at the bad weather, which interfered with her washing, lived in unbroken sulkiness. She treated him worse than a dog, and it was truly with the patience of a dog that he endured everything, so much did he fear being sent away. A plan of vengeance had arisen in his brain, and slowly, during the months, ever since he had learned that his case was incurable, his project had absorbed his entire mental activity,--indeed, his whole existence. He breathed only for his plan, for the sure, propitious opportunity.

At last it came, and a terrible day it was. At dusk his daughter had left, closing the door, as was her habit, and had not returned at night. The old man was parched with thirst and his physical torture had doubled. He resolved upon quick action.

In the morning,--it might have been about seven o'clock--his daughter returned, or rather, rolled into the room, and with her, pell-mell came "Jane", Bernardo's "friend". Jane was roundly berating his daughter. "You rotten thing!" she cried. "I'll show you! Trying to take away somebody else's man." And the two women came to blows, rousing the entire neighborhood. They tried at last to separate the combatants, but it would have been easier to break them to bits, so fiercely did they struggle against each other. There was a whistle; the police arrived, and the women were taken to the lock-up. All this as quick as a flash.

The old man had not had time to utter a word. But an extreme rage, blind,--an anger such as only savage beasts can know, overpowered him. What! His daughter, the mistress of Bernardo! This was the last straw!

Towards noon the mulatto came back. He had spent the night away from home, under the pretext of a special patrol; he returned, ignorant of the morning's events. He came in smiling, in that measured walk of his, waddling along. He approached Felix and asked him the classic question: "Now then, how goes it?"

Felix did not reply and merely made a sign with his hand. The policeman entered. When he had come near, Felix said to him in a low voice that he had something very serious to tell him. But first of all he insisted that Bernardo go and bring his large knife.

"Why that, Felix? What do you want to do with a knife?" asked the other.

The old man smiled mysteriously. "Quick, my boy, I'll tell you afterwards, and you'll see that my story will be worth the trouble."

"All right, I'll get it," replied the officer. And a minute later he was back with the knife, which he gave to the invalid.

"Now," continued the latter, "go and close the door, so that nobody will hear. Close it well, and turn the key."

Bernardo felt some mistrust at all this mystery, but knowing for certain that the helpless old man could do him no harm, he obeyed, curiously waiting to learn what the other was up to.

"So, you want to tell me now?--Not yet! Here, first put this watch in your pocket." And the old man drew from his pocket an ancient nickel watch which he gave to the *cabra*.

"What am I to do with this, Felix?" asked the mulatto.

"Keep it, I tell you," was the reply.

"The old duffer is crazy for sure," thought Bernardo, nevertheless doing as he was told. Then, seeing in what manner the invalid had grasped the knife he discreetly withdrew a few paces.

Well, almost immediately Felix made a sudden movement that caused his pain to increase anew, and he began to groan, to utter most terrible cries, almost shrieks.

"I am dying! I am dying!"

Bernardo had never heard such awful groaning; his mistrust grew, and, seeing that the old man still clutched the knife, he thought the invalid would kill him if he should attempt to approach. He therefore again stepped back a few paces and awaited developments, persuaded that he had a lunatic in front of him. The groaning became louder and louder, so that it was easily to be heard outside. Finally, the *cabra*, tired of waiting, said, "I'll be back right away, Felix." And he was about to leave.

Brusquely, the old man uncovered his own breast, and with a rapid movement, right over the heart, he thrust in the blade with all his might, up to the hilt. Not a drop of blood spurted out, the thick blade obstructing the wound. His face convulsed with an expression of excruciating torment; his hanging arms grew rigid.

The officer rushed to the door, opened it, called for help and returned to pull the knife from the wound, and to see whether it was yet possible to save the unfortunate man. Men and women, wildly excited, ran up to the house crying loudly, and, seeing this man with a long knife whence the blood was dripping, seeing also the pierced breast of old Felix, the whole populace rushed upon Bernardo, disarmed him, crying "Kill him! Kill him!" Bernardo was punched and kicked and cudgelled from one infuriated person to the other in the crowd, and led to the police-station by a multitude which every moment waxed greater and more threatening.

Several months later the trial came to an end. Bernardo was sentenced to hard labor for life. Nobody would believe his story. The proofs were overwhelming. Had he not been caught red-handed? The presence of the nickel-watch in his pocket indicated sufficiently that the motive of the crime was robbery. The vengeance of old Felix had been well calculated: the result was there. The old man had conquered.

THE PIGEONS
By Coelho Netto

Member Brazilian Academy of Letters

When the pigeons leave, misfortune follows.
                --Indian superstition.

When Joanna appeared at the door yawning, fatigued after the long sleepless night spent at her son's bedside, Triburcio, on the terrace, leaning against his spade, was watching the pigeon-house closely.

The sun was already setting and gilded the moist leaves. At the edge of the ravine, turtle-doves and starlings were circling in the air, making a joyous noise above the high branches of the neighboring trees.

The *caboclo* [6] Indian did not remove his eyes from the pigeon-house. The wrinkles on his forehead bore witness to an inner struggle--, grave thoughts which were clouding his spirit. A pigeon took to flight, then another, and still another; he turned his head, following them with his gaze until they were out of sight, and then returned to his melancholy contemplation.

[6] Caboclo signifies copper-colored. Indigenous tribes of Brazil   are so called from the color of their skin.

The birds came and went, entered the pigeon-house and left in agitated manner, cooing loudly; they circled above the dwelling, sought the trees, alighted on the thatch of the cabin, descended to earth in spiral flight.

Some seemed to be getting their bearings, to seek a route: they gazed across the clear stretches of space and penetrated to the distant horizons. Others would fly off, describing vast circles, and would return to the pigeon-house. Then all would come together as if for a discussion, to plan their departure.

Some, undecided, opened their wings as if about to fly away, but soon would close them again. Still others would dart off, only to come back aimlessly, and the noise increased to a hubbub of hurried leaving.

The Indian gazed fixedly. Well he knew that the life of his little son was at stake, and depended upon the decision of the birds. "When the pigeons leave, misfortune quickly follows."

Joanna noticed his preoccupation. "What is the matter?" she asked.

The *caboclo* scratched his head and made no reply. The woman insisted. "What is the trouble, Tiburcio?"

"The pigeons have taken a whim into their heads, Joanna."

"And you are lost in the contemplation of it? I have not cared to speak, but I know well the meaning of what I see."

The *caboclo* slung the spade across his shoulder and walked slowly up the road that led to the plantation, through the wet hay which exhaled a piquant odor.

Some hens were clucking, hidden in the high grass, and a little ribbon of water which flowed gently along sparkled here and there through the openings in the brushwood.

Tiburcio, head bowed, spade on his shoulder, could not shake off the deep impression that had been made upon him by the sudden migration of the birds.

It was the fatal sign.

To be sure, he had heard the owl's screech for many and many a night; but he had seen no cause for fear in this: everything was going along nicely; their little son was in good health and they, too, knew no illness. But now the warning of the evil omen was confirmed. The pigeons which he had himself brought up were flying away. They were leaving, thus forecasting the arrival of death.

He turned back; he raised his eyes. There were the birds high above, still circling about, and Joanna was at the threshold of the cabin, leaning against the jamb, her arms crossed, her head hanging. The poor woman was surely weeping.

Within him he felt a mute explosion of hatred and revolt against the ungrateful birds. Never had he had the courage to kill a single one of them. He lived only for the purpose of keeping the pigeon-house in order, thinking only of making it larger so that it might accommodate more pairs. And the little child, was it not he who crushed the millet for the fledglings, who climbed the mango-tree, going from branch to branch to see whether there wasn't some crack through which the rain came in? Who knows? Perhaps the pigeons were leaving their dwelling because they no longer saw him?

He shrugged his shoulders and continued on his way. As he crossed the dam his heart palpitated wildly. He stopped. The water, held back in its course, threw back a motionless reflection of him. But although he looked down upon it he saw not his image; his thoughts were entirely with the little child who, burning with fever, was in delirium.

He chose a side path. The millet stems were so high that he disappeared within them with a crumpling of dry leaves. The soft ant-hills which it was his daily custom to level off failed to attract his attention. He walked straight on. Parrots flew by, chattering, with their green wings shining in the sun, and huge grasshoppers were jumping in the leaves.

He came upon a straw hut,--here the child was wont to play with its toys;-- there was even now a boot of wild sugar-cane. But already the grass was beginning to invade the abandoned shelter.... For a month the little child had not visited the place. When the father came to the field of manioc he sat down, bent almost in two. The spade weighed upon his shoulders like a burden. The strength had oozed out of his legs. His whole body was broken with fatigue, as if at the end of a long journey. He sat down upon a hillock and began to trace lines upon the earth, with a distraught air.

At times it seemed as if he heard the echo of his wife's voice. He would raise his head and strain his ears to catch the sound. But only the rustling of the leaves stirred by the breeze and the chirping of the insects in the sun came to him. All earth seemed to perspire. A diaphanous vapor rose tremblingly from the hot soil; the leaves hung languidly, and through the intense blueness of the sky passed some *urubus* [7] in search of distant lodgings.

[7] Urubu: the black vulture of South America.

Suddenly a pigeon winged through the air, then another, and still another. They were leaving ... they were leaving!... A beating of wings,--more on the way. They would never return, never! They were fleeing in horror, feeling the approach of death.

For a long time he gazed about him, but could see only the rich verdure waving to the wind in the warm transparency of the atmosphere. He should have taken his child to town as soon as the illness had appeared. But who could have foretold this? He raised his eyes to heaven and they lingered upon the luminous azure; then came another pigeon. He shook his head and, striking his fist against his thigh, slung his spade back upon his shoulder and turned in the direction of his house.

When Joanna saw him on the terrace she appeared to divine his thoughts.

"It is well you returned, my dear! All alone here I am at a loss as to what to do."

He looked at the pigeon-house, saw that it was deserted, and ominously silent. As evening fell Tiburcio sat down upon the threshold of the cabin and began to smoke, waiting for the pigeons. The grasshoppers were shrilling; all the birds who had their nests in the tree nearby retired and, as it was still light, they lingered in the branches to trill their good-night cadences.

The sky grew pale. The landscape was veiled in a light mist. The evening breeze scattered the gentle odor of lilies. Not very far off a dog barked now and then. At times a grave lowing saddened the silence. Tiburcio did not remove his eyes from the pigeon-house, unless it was to pierce the shadows and try to discover in the distance one of the birds. Perhaps some of them would return.

Where could they find a better shelter? The forest was full of dangers and domestic pigeons could scarcely live in the brushwood. What other pigeon-roost could have attracted them? If he had but followed the line of their flight ... Some had taken the direction of the fields, others had flown towards the mountains, and there was no sign of any returning.

It was now quite dark. Joanna lighted a candle. Already the frogs were croaking in the marshes. A star shone in the sky. Tiburcio fixed his gaze upon it and began to pray in low tones. The silence was scarcely broken by the murmuring of the water as it ran and broke over the stones in the ravine not far away, just behind the cabin.

Tiburcio sighed, arose, leaned against the jamb and lacked courage to go inside. Joanna came near the door.

"And now?"

"The same thing," he replied.

He stepped down, called her, and together they went towards the terrace. Near the mango-tree, directly under the pigeon-house, they stopped, and the Indian, as if in fear of being heard by the child, asked softly, "Joanna, don't you know any prayers for this?" And he pointed to the deserted pigeon-roost.

"Only Lina knows," she answered.

"She can pronounce the proper spells?"

"So they say."

Tiburcio stood as if in a dream. Suddenly, in a firm voice, he announced, "I am going to her."

"Now?"

"Certainly!... Haven't you just said that she was a sorceress?"

"I have never seen it, Tiburcio.... That's what people say."

"But you?"

"I? No. And I am afraid that it is too late. You have seen your self how far gone he is! He is no longer interested in anything. I move about, I speak, I go here and there, I come back again into the room,--but it is all nothing to him. Ah! God in heaven!"

Her voice died out Suddenly she melted into tears. Tiburcio withdrew and commenced to pace slowly up and down the terrace. The white moon was rising. The fields became less obscure and, in the light, the shadows of the trees, very black, stretched across the ground.

"Patience, dear woman, patience!"

The strident crickets were chirping. The *caboclo* murmured, "Yes, I know ..."

Of a sudden Joanna shuddered. Quivering she turned towards the cabin, from whose wide door shone a ray of livid light; for a moment her astonished gaze lingered and then, with a bound she was gone.

Tiburcio, motionless, without understanding what his wife had just done, quietly awaited her return, when a piercing cry rang out. The *caboclo* rushed to the cabin and made for the room where the candle was burning. The woman, on her knees before the little bed, leaning over the child, was sobbing desperately.

"What has happened, Joanna?"

She gave a hoarse cry and threw her arms across the corpse of her son.

"Look! It's all over!"

She bent down, her face brushed a cheek that was burning; her trembling hands felt a little body that was still aflame. She touched the sunken chest, where the ribs showed through like laths, and the hollow abdomen.

"Listen to his heart, Tiburcio!"

He could only reply, "It is all over!"

The mother arose with a leap, disfigured, her hair dishevelled, her eyes sparkling. She tried to speak, stretched her hands out to her husband, but fell limp upon a basket and, bowed down, bathed in tears, she began to repeat the name of her son with an infinite tenderness that was rent by sobs.

"My Luiz! My little Luiz! But a moment ago living, oh blessed Virgin!"

Tiburcio turned away and in the room, before the table, he stopped, his eyes wandering, his lips trembling, the tears rolling in big drops down his bony face. Joanna left the chamber, wavering as if drunk, and seeing him, threw herself into his arms; he held her without uttering a word, and they stood thus in embrace for a long time, in the dark, narrow room where the crickets were chirping.

Joanna went back to the chamber. Tiburcio remained leaning against the table, his eyes fixed upon the candle which flickered in the breeze. Slowly the light of the moon came in, white, climbing upon the walls. He arose with a sigh, went to the door, sat down upon the threshold, lighted his pipe and looked leisurely out upon the country, which was growing brighter beneath the moon. Suddenly it seemed to him that he heard the cooing of pigeons. Above, the stars were shining, the tree tops glittered in the moonlight. Could it be an illusion?

Motionless, he concentrated his attention. The cooing continued. He arose impetuously, walked straight to the pigeon-roost and leaned against the trunk of the mango-tree.

"Could it be the pigeons who were returning after the passing of death?" he began to mutter in fury, replying to his thoughts. "Now it's too late! A curse upon them!"

A beating of wings, a tender cooing, and little cries came from the pigeon-house. There was no doubt now. He went forward and, from the middle of the terrace watched the pigeon-house, walking resolutely towards the cabin.

Joanna was sobbing hopelessly. He took the candle, went to the kitchen, and seeing the axe in a corner he seized it, still muttering. He then turned back to the terrace and, having reached the mango-tree, rolled up the sleeves of his coarse shirt so that he might swing the axe.

At the first blow against the post which supported the pigeon-house the birds grew still. Tiburcio redoubled his efforts. A crack now weakened the structure, but still it resisted. He leaned the axe against the trunk and, grasping the branches, raised himself to the top of the tree. From there he supported himself between two boughs and gave the large box a furious kick. The pigeon-roost fell shattered to the ground.

Two pigeons flew off in great fright, dazed. Uncertain of their direction in the clearness of the night, they lit upon the roof of the hut.

The *caboclo* slid down lightly along the trunk and saw two little bodies who were whining, staggering, dragging themselves along. They were two little pigeons. He bent over them, took them in his hands and began to examine them. They were ugly, still without wings, having only a thin down to cover the muscles of their soft, wrinkled bodies. The Indian turned them over this way and that in his shrivelled hands. He felt their fragile bones, and the little things struggled to fly away, moving the stumps of their wings; they stretched out their necks and whined.

Gnashing his teeth, Tiburcio squeezed the fledglings and crushed them. Their tender bones cracked like bits of wood. The blood gushed forth and trickled, warm, through the tightened fingers of the man.

Under the impulse of his fury he threw them to the ground; they flattened out, soft as rotten fruit. And the *caboclo*, growling to himself, trampled upon them. The parent-birds were cooing dolorously upon the thatched roof, flying hither and thither.

Joanna, embracing her dead child, was still sobbing when Tiburcio entered the chamber. He stopped before the little bed, and looked down. Of a sudden the woman shook, arose with a start, seized her husband's arm, her eyes distended and her mouth wide open, her head bending over as if to hear voices, faraway sounds.

"What is it, Joanna? What is the matter with you?"

In terror she stammered reply. "The pigeons, dear husband. Don't you hear them?"

It was their sad cooing that came from the roof of the house. "They are returning! Who knows? He is yet warm!" she cried.

And in the heart of the woman arose a great hope.

Tiburcio shrugged his shoulders.

"Now it's their turn to mourn!" he answered. "They are sobbing, like us. It's a pair that remained behind because of the little ones. I dashed the pigeon-house to earth, I have killed the fledglings. See!"

And he showed his bloody hands.

"They flew away; they're on the house. Do you want to see?"

He went out; she followed. They walked to the terrace. Tiburcio pointed to the ruined pigeon-house. Then he grasped the crushed bodies of the little birds. "Look!"

Without breathing a word Joanna looked on. In her horror she had stopped weeping. She gazed upon her husband, whose burning eyes flashed fire. He threw the first little pigeon upon the roof bellowing, "'T is well!"

He threw the second.

"'T is well!" he repeated.

The pigeons, frightened, flew off into the dark foliage.

"'T is well," he said once more.

Joanna, dumb, terrified, could not remove her eyes from her husband, who was now crying with sobs, his opened hands stained with blood.

"Come, dear husband. It was the will of God. Our little son is in heaven!" And slowly she heartened him. They entered their cabin and, before the pallet of the dead child, the tears gushed from their eyes, while, on the roof above, the pigeons, who had returned, were cooing dolorously.

AUNT ZEZE'S TEARS
By Carmen Dolores

(Emilia Moncorva Bandeira de Mello, 1852-1910)

Pale and thin, for eighteen years she had lived with her youngest sister, who had married very early and now possessed five children: two young ladies of marriageable age, a third still in short dresses, and two little boys. Maria-Jose, whose nickname was Zeze, had never been beautiful or winning. Upon her father's death it was thought best that she should go to live with her sister Engracigna's family. Here she led a monotonous existence, helping to bring up her nephews and nieces, who were born in that young and happy household with a regularity that brooked small intervals between the births.

A long, pointed nose disfigured her face, and her lips, extremely thin, looked like a pale crack. Her thoughtful gaze alone possessed a certain melancholy attractiveness. But even here, her eyes, protruding too far for the harmony of the lines upon her face seemed always to be red, and her brows narrow and sparse.

Of late, an intricate network of wrinkles as fine as hairs, had formed at the corner of her eyes. From her nose, likewise, two furrows ran along the transparent delicacy of her skin and reached either side of her mouth. When she smiled, these wrinkles would cover her countenance with a mask of premature age, and threatened soon to disfigure her entirely. And yet, from habit, and through passive obedience to routine, Maria-Jose continued to dress like a young girl of eighteen, in brightly colored gowns, thin waists and white hats that ill became her frail and oldish face.

She would remain for a long time in painful indecision when it was a matter of picking out some piece of goods that was of too bright a red or blue,--as if instinctively she understood the disharmony of these hues with her age, whose rapid oncoming they moreover placed in all the more noticeable contrast. And at such times Engracigna and her daughters would say to her with a vehemence whose effect they little guessed, "Why, Zeze! Buy something and be done with it!... How silly! Do you want to dress like a widow? What a notion!"

And at bottom they meant it.

None of them saw Maria-Jose as she really was. Living with her day by day had served to efface the actual appearance of the faded old maid. For, in the minds of the mother and her daughters, who were moreover of a frivolous and indifferent sort, Zeze had grown to be the type, very vague, to be sure, but the eternal type of young girl of marriagable years who always should be well dressed and smiling.

When she would be out walking with her nieces, of sixteen and seventeen years, who wore the same clothes as she herself did, but whose graceful and lively charm became their gay colors of youth so well, Zeze's intelligence saw only too plainly the contrast between her and them; she would hold aloof from the laughing set, morose, wounded, as if oppressed by an unspeakable shame.

Ah! Who can depict the secret chagrin of an old maid who sees pass by in useless monotony her dark, loveless, despairing days, without hope even of some event of personal interest, while about her moves the busy whirl of happier creatures whose life has but one goal, who feel emotions and tendernesses, and who look upon her simply as an obscure accessory in the household's affairs! They all loved her, of course, but not one of them suspected that she, too, could cherish those aspirations that are common to all human beings.

Her self-denial seemed to be a most natural thing; indeed, they hardly considered her in the light of a living person; she was no longer of any consequence.

This was an attitude that satisfied the general egotism of the family, and to which they all had grown accustomed, never suspecting the grievous aspect of her sacrifice which was hidden by a sentiment of proud dignity.

So, when they would go to the theatre, and the box held only five--Engracigna, her husband, Fabio, and the three young ladies,--Maria-Jose knew beforehand that her sister, snugly wrapped in her opera-cloak, would come to her and say gently, in that purring voice of hers: "You'll stay at home with the children tonight, won't you, Zeze? Little Paul isn't very well, and I wouldn't think of leaving him with anybody else...."

And she would remain behind, without betraying the revolt within her which, upon each occasion of these evidences of selfishness, would make the anemic blood in her veins tremble with agitation.

Alone in the dining-room she would ply her needle mechanically, while her nephews would amuse themselves with the toys scattered upon the table,--colored pictures and lead soldiers. Every other moment they would call her.

"Aunt Zeze, look at George pinching me!"

"I am not! Paul hit me first!..."

And the good aunt would quiet them. Then, after both had been put to sleep in their little twin beds, she would rest her elbows upon the window-sill of her gloomy old-maid's room, and placing both hands beneath her sharp chin, her gaze directed towards heaven, she would lose herself in contemplation of the stars that shone in the limpid sky, less lonely, surely, than she upon earth. In vain did her eyes seek in the eyes of another that expression of sympathy and tenderness which alone would console her....

The truth is that Maria-Jose was suffering from the disappointment of unrequited passion. She had fallen in love with Monjardin, a poet and great friend of her brother-in-law, Fabio. Monjardin came to the house every Sunday.

Older than she, almost forty, but having preserved all the attractiveness of youth,--a black moustache, a vigorous, yet graceful figure, eyes still bright, charming and wide-awake,--Monjardin, without knowing it, had conquered Zeze.

This had come about in a rather curious manner. Finding the conversation of Fabio's wife and daughters too commonplace, Monjardin, when he would recite some of his poems or tell some story connected with his literary life, preferred to address Maria-Jose, whom he saw to be of a serious and impressive nature.

"Let's have another poem, please, Mr. Monjardin!" she would ask in supplicating tone. "For instance, that one you call 'Regrets.' You know?"

And then he would describe in his verse the grief of a heart, disillusioned and broken by the cruelties of fate, that evoked in vain the remembrance of yesterday's lost loves, vanished in the mists of eternal despair.

He recited these bitter griefs in a strong, healthy man's voice, erect in the center of the parlor, looking mechanically, distractedly at Maria-Jose with his dreamy eyes; the concentrated effort of his memory brought to his face an involuntary immobility which Maria-Jose, most deliciously touched, drank in.

The poet had announced that he had written a poem which he would recite at Zeze's anniversary dinner. The date for this was but a few days distant, and ever since the poet's announcement the whole family had taken to teasing the old maid, christening her "the muse of inspiration," and asking her when the wedding would take place....

She smiled ingenuously; at such times her face would even take on an air of unusual happiness; her features grew animated, less wrinkled and more firm.

On the day of the celebration Maria-Jose came out of her room radiant with hope. At the belt of her white dress bloomed a rose; a little blood, set pulsing by her agitated heart, brought a feeble color to her marble cheeks, from which now protruded her long nose in a manner less displeasing than usual.

"See, mamma," remarked one of the nieces, "doesn't Zeze look like a young girl today?"

They dined amidst merry chatter. Seated directly across from Monjardin, Maria-Jose, hiding her glances behind the fruit-bowls that covered the table, looked at him furtively without surfeit. Her poor heart beat as if it would burst, waiting in agonized suspense for the poem in which the poet, without doubt, was to declare his intimate feelings for her. Monjardin had already pointed to his pocket as a token that he had the verses with him, and Zeze had trembled with gratification as she bashfully lowered her long face.

Champagne sparkled in the glasses and toasts were given. Several guests of distinction spoke first, then followed the hosts and their children,--frolicsome little things. Finally Monjardin arose and unfolded a manuscript, asking permission to declaim the verses which he had composed in honor of Maria-Jose, the central figure of the occasion. The guests greeted his remarks with noisy and enthusiastic approbation.

"Hear! Hear!"

Engracigna and her daughters leaned over and cast malicious glances in the direction of Maria-Jose, but she was paying no attention to them. Her ears were buzzing; it seemed that everything was turning round.

Monjardin, the center of all eyes, made pompous preparation; he pulled down his vest, arranged his sleeves and, in sonorous, cadenced voice began to recite his alexandrines, scanning the lines impeccably.

His poem opened with a eulogy of the ineffable virtue, compounded of self-abnegation and chastity, that distinguished the angelic creature who, with her white tutelary wings, watched over the happiness of his dear friend's love nest. He then recalled that the date of this day commemorated the happy birth of a being of immaculate purity, Maria-Jose, a veritable saint who had renounced all her own aspirations so that she might consecrate herself entirely to the duties of her sister's family; gentle figure of the mother-guardian, who would soon be the beloved grandmother sharing with her sister the joys of younger households which would soon be formed, offsprings of that home which her devoted tenderness as aunt and sister at present cultivated. As he came to a close, the poet raised his cup of sparkling wine and, in exalted voice, drank to the health of Zeze amidst the loud huzzahs of all present.

"Long live Aunt Zeze! Hurrah for Aunt Zeze!" cried the children, glass in hand, while the nieces laughed loudly, blushing to the ears, for they had understood very well the poet's reference to future "younger households."

Fabio and his wife, their eyes somewhat brightened by the strong champagne, proposed in turn their toast to Zeze.

"Here's to Zeze and the eighteen happy years we've lived together!..."

Maria-Jose, as soon as she had seized the significance of Monjardin's verses, had grown deathly pale; stricken by sudden disillusionment, she felt a glacial chill overwhelm her body to the very marrow; she feared that she would faint straightway and provide a spectacle for the guests, who were all drinking her health, their eyes focussed upon her. A veil of tears spread before her sight.... In vain she tried to repress them, to force a smile of thanks upon her face. The smile wrinkled into a dolorous grimace; she succeeded only in convulsing her contracted visage with the sobs that she sought to restrain. Overcome at last, humiliated, powerless, she broke into tears, and this unforeseen denouement put an end at once to all the pleasure of the dinner.

"Zeze! Zeze! What ails you?..."

Engracigna had rushed to her side in alarm; everyone rose, seeking the reason for the outburst; they surrounded the poor creature, whose head had sunk upon the table, in the midst of the rose petals, the fruits and the glasses which were strewn in charming confusion.

"What is the trouble?..."

A nervous attack, perhaps?... Confusion produced in her by the touching poem?...

Finally they raised Maria-Jose's head and bathed it in cool water; whereupon the face of the poor old maid stood revealed in all the ugliness that her spasms of convulsive weeping cast over it, with her large aquiline nose, her protruding eyes and her livid lips ...

And now Monjardin drew near. Delicately raising the icy fingers of Maria-Jose he lifted them to the edge of his perfumed moustache and placed upon them a grateful kiss; then, turning to Engracigna's daughters he said, with a solemn, self-complacent tone, "Aunt Zeze's tears are the most beautiful homage that could be rendered to my poor verses."

The Codes Of Hammurabi And Moses
W. W. Davies

QTY

The discovery of the Hammurabi Code is one of the greatest achievements of archaeology, and is of paramount interest, not only to the student of the Bible, but also to all those interested in ancient history...

Religion   ISBN: *1-59462-338-4*   Pages:132
                                    MSRP $12.95

The Theory of Moral Sentiments
Adam Smith

QTY

This work from 1749. contains original theories of conscience amd moral judgment and it is the foundation for systemof morals.

Philosophy ISBN: *1-59462-777-0*   Pages:536
                                    MSRP $19.95

Jessica's First Prayer
Hesba Stretton

QTY

In a screened and secluded corner of one of the many railway-bridges which span the streets of London there could be seen a few years ago, from five o'clock every morning until half past eight, a tidily set-out coffee-stall, consisting of a trestle and board, upon which stood two large tin cans, with a small fire of charcoal burning under each so as to keep the coffee boiling during the early hours of the morning when the work-people were thronging into the city on their way to their daily toil...

Childrens   ISBN: *1-59462-373-2*   Pages:84
                                    MSRP $9.95

My Life and Work
Henry Ford

QTY

Henry Ford revolutionized the world with his implementation of mass production for the Model T automobile. Gain valuable business insight into his life and work with his own auto-biography... "We have only started on our development of our country we have not as yet, with all our talk of wonderful progress, done more than scratch the surface. The progress has been wonderful enough but..."

Biographies/   ISBN: *1-59462-198-5*   Pages:300
                                    MSRP $21.95

www.bookjungle.com *email: sales@bookjungle.com fax: 630-214-0564 mail: Book Jungle PO Box 2226 Champaign, IL 61825*

The Art of Cross-Examination
Francis Wellman

QTY

I presume it is the experience of every author, after his first book is published upon an important subject, to be almost overwhelmed with a wealth of ideas and illustrations which could readily have been included in his book, and which to his own mind, at least, seem to make a second edition inevitable. Such certainly was the case with me; and when the first edition had reached its sixth impression in five months, I rejoiced to learn that it seemed to my publishers that the book had met with a sufficiently favorable reception to justify a second and considerably enlarged edition. ..

Reference   **ISBN: *1-59462-647-2***   **Pages:412**   *MSRP $19.95*

On the Duty of Civil Disobedience
Henry David Thoreau

QTY

Thoreau wrote his famous essay, On the Duty of Civil Disobedience, as a protest against an unjust but popular war and the immoral but popular institution of slave-owning. He did more than write—he declined to pay his taxes, and was hauled off to gaol in consequence. Who can say how much this refusal of his hastened the end of the war and of slavery ?

Law   **ISBN: *1-59462-747-9***   **Pages:48**   *MSRP $7.45*

Dream Psychology Psychoanalysis for Beginners
Sigmund Freud

QTY

Sigmund Freud, born Sigismund Schlomo Freud (May 6, 1856 - September 23, 1939), was a Jewish-Austrian neurologist and psychiatrist who co-founded the psychoanalytic school of psychology. Freud is best known for his theories of the unconscious mind, especially involving the mechanism of repression; his redefinition of sexual desire as mobile and directed towards a wide variety of objects; and his therapeutic techniques, especially his understanding of transference in the therapeutic relationship and the presumed value of dreams as sources of insight into unconscious desires.

Dream Psychology
Psychoanalysis for Beginners

Sigmund Freud

Psychology   **ISBN: *1-59462-905-6***   **Pages:196**   *MSRP $15.45*

The Miracle of Right Thought
Orison Swett Marden

QTY

Believe with all of your heart that you will do what you were made to do. When the mind has once formed the habit of holding cheerful, happy, prosperous pictures, it will not be easy to form the opposite habit. It does not matter how improbable or how far away this realization may see, or how dark the prospects may be, if we visualize them as best we can, as vividly as possible, hold tenaciously to them and vigorously struggle to attain them, they will gradually become actualized, realized in the life. But a desire, a longing without endeavor, a yearning abandoned or held indifferently will vanish without realization.

Self Help   **ISBN: *1-59462-644-8***   **Pages:360**   *MSRP $25.45*

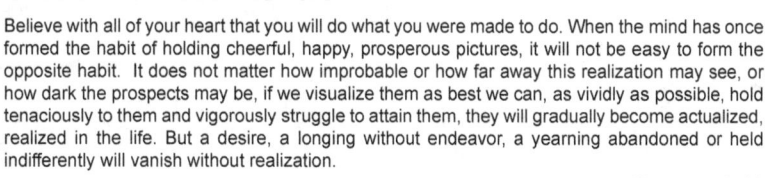

QTY

The Rosicrucian Cosmo-Conception Mystic Christianity by *Max Heindel*　ISBN: *1-59462-188-8*　**$38.95**
The Rosicrucian Cosmo-conception is not dogmatic, neither does it appeal to any other authority than the reason of the student. It is: not controversial, but is: sent forth in the, hope that it may help to clear...　New Age/Religion Pages 646

Abandonment To Divine Providence by *Jean-Pierre de Caussade*　ISBN: *1-59462-228-0*　**$25.95**
"The Rev. Jean Pierre de Caussade was one of the most remarkable spiritual writers of the Society of Jesus in France in the 18th Century. His death took place at Toulouse in 1751. His works have gone through many editions and have been republished...　Inspirational/Religion Pages 400

Mental Chemistry by *Charles Haanel*　ISBN: *1-59462-192-6*　**$23.95**
Mental Chemistry allows the change of material conditions by combining and appropriately utilizing the power of the mind. Much like applied chemistry creates something new and unique out of careful combinations of chemicals the mastery of mental chemistry...　New Age Pages 354

The Letters of Robert Browning and Elizabeth Barret Barrett 1845-1846 vol II　ISBN: *1-59462-193-4*　**$35.95**
by *Robert Browning and Elizabeth Barrett*　Biographies Pages 596

Gleanings In Genesis (volume I) by *Arthur W. Pink*　ISBN: *1-59462-130-6*　**$27.45**
Appropriately has Genesis been termed "the seed plot of the Bible" for in it we have, in germ form, almost all of the great doctrines which are afterwards fully developed in the books of Scripture which follow...　Religion/Inspirational Pages 420

The Master Key by *L. W. de Laurence*　ISBN: *1-59462-001-6*　**$30.95**
In no branch of human knowledge has there been a more lively increase of the spirit of research during the past few years than in the study of Psychology, Concentration and Mental Discipline. The requests for authentic lessons in Thought Control, Mental Discipline and...　New Age/Business Pages 422

The Lesser Key Of Solomon Goetia by *L. W. de Laurence*　ISBN: *1-59462-092-X*　**$9.95**
This translation of the first book of the "Lernegton" which is now for the first time made accessible to students of Talismanic Magic was done, after careful collation and edition, from numerous Ancient Manuscripts in Hebrew, Latin, and French...　New Age/Occult Pages 92

Rubaiyat Of Omar Khayyam by *Edward Fitzgerald*　ISBN: *1-59462-332-5*　**$13.95**
Edward Fitzgerald, whom the world has already learned, in spite of his own efforts to remain within the shadow of anonymity, to look upon as one of the rarest poets of the century, was born at Bredfield, in Suffolk, on the 31st of March, 1809. He was the third son of John Purcell...　Music Pages 172

Ancient Law by *Henry Maine*　ISBN: *1-59462-128-4*　**$29.95**
The chief object of the following pages is to indicate some of the earliest ideas of mankind, as they are reflected in Ancient Law, and to point out the relation of those ideas to modern thought.　Religiom/History Pages 452

Far-Away Stories by *William J. Locke*　ISBN: *1-59462-129-2*　**$19.45**
"Good wine needs no bush, but a collection of mixed vintages does. And this book is just such a collection. Some of the stories I do not want to remain buried for ever in the museum files of dead magazine-numbers an author's not unpardonable vanity..."　Fiction Pages 272

Life of David Crockett by *David Crockett*　ISBN: *1-59462-250-7*　**$27.45**
"Colonel David Crockett was one of the most remarkable men of the times in which he lived. Born in humble life, but gifted with a strong will, an indomitable courage, and unremitting perseverance...　Biographies/New Age Pages 424

Lip-Reading by *Edward Nitchie*　ISBN: *1-59462-206-X*　**$25.95**
Edward B. Nitchie, founder of the New York School for the Hard of Hearing, now the Nitchie School of Lip-Reading, Inc, wrote "LIP-READING Principles and Practice". The development and perfecting of this meritorious work on lip-reading was an undertaking...　How-to Pages 400

A Handbook of Suggestive Therapeutics, Applied Hypnotism, Psychic Science　ISBN: *1-59462-214-0*　**$24.95**
by *Henry Munro*　Health/New Age/Health/Self-help Pages 376

A Doll's House: and Two Other Plays by *Henrik Ibsen*　ISBN: *1-59462-112-8*　**$19.95**
Henrik Ibsen created this classic when in revolutionary 1848 Rome. Introducing some striking concepts in playwriting for the realist genre, this play has been studied the world over.　Fiction/Classics/Plays 308

The Light of Asia by *sir Edwin Arnold*　ISBN: *1-59462-204-3*　**$13.95**
In this poetic masterpiece, Edwin Arnold describes the life and teachings of Buddha. The man who was to become known as Buddha to the world was born as Prince Gautama of India but he rejected the worldly riches and abandoned the reigns of power when...　Religion/History/Biographies Pages 170

The Complete Works of Guy de Maupassant by *Guy de Maupassant*　ISBN: *1-59462-157-8*　**$16.95**
"For days and days, nights and nights, I had dreamed of that first kiss which was to consecrate our engagement, and I knew not on what spot I should put my lips..."　Fiction/Classics Pages 240

The Art of Cross-Examination by *Francis L. Wellman*　ISBN: *1-59462-309-0*　**$26.95**
Written by a renowned trial lawyer, Wellman imparts his experience and uses case studies to explain how to use psychology to extract desired information through questioning.　How-to/Science/Reference Pages 408

Answered or Unanswered? by *Louisa Vaughan*　ISBN: *1-59462-248-5*　**$10.95**
Miracles of Faith in China　Religion Pages 112

The Edinburgh Lectures on Mental Science (1909) by *Thomas*　ISBN: *1-59462-008-3*　**$11.95**
This book contains the substance of a course of lectures recently given by the writer in the Queen Street Hall, Edinburgh. Its purpose is to indicate the Natural Principles governing the relation between Mental Action and Material Conditions...　New Age/Psychology Pages 148

Ayesha by *H. Rider Haggard*　ISBN: *1-59462-301-5*　**$24.95**
Verily and indeed it is the unexpected that happens! Probably if there was one person upon the earth from whom the Editor of this, and of a certain previous history, did not expect to hear again...　Classics Pages 380

Ayala's Angel by *Anthony Trollope*　ISBN: *1-59462-352-X*　**$29.95**
The two girls were both pretty, but Lucy who was twenty-one who supposed to be simple and comparatively unattractive, whereas Ayala was credited, as her Bombwhat romantic name might show, with poetic charm and a taste for romance. Ayala when her father died was nineteen...　Fiction Pages 484

The American Commonwealth by *James Bryce*　ISBN: *1-59462-286-8*　**$34.45**
An interpretation of American democratic political theory. It examines political mechanics and society from the perspective of Scotsman James Bryce　Politics Pages 572

Stories of the Pilgrims by *Margaret P. Pumphrey*　ISBN: *1-59462-116-0*　**$17.95**
This book explores pilgrims religious oppression in England as well as their escape to Holland and eventual crossing to America on the Mayflower, and their early days in New England...　History Pages 268

QTY

The Fasting Cure *by Sinclair Upton* ISBN: *1-59462-222-1* **$13.95**
In the Cosmopolitan Magazine for May, 1910, and in the Contemporary Review (London) for April, 1910, I published an article dealing with my experiences in fasting. I have written a great many magazine articles, but never one which attracted so much attention... New Age/Self Help/Health Pages 164

Hebrew Astrology *by Sepharial* ISBN: *1-59462-308-2* **$13.45**
In these days of advanced thinking it is a matter of common observation that we have left many of the old landmarks behind and that we are now pressing forward to greater heights and to a wider horizon than that which represented the mind-content of our progenitors... Astrology Pages 144

Thought Vibration or The Law of Attraction in the Thought World ISBN: *1-59462-127-6* **$12.95**

by William Walker Atkinson Psychology/Religion Pages 144

Optimism *by Helen Keller* ISBN: *1-59462-108-X* **$15.95**
Helen Keller was blind, deaf, and mute since 19 months old, yet famously learned how to overcome these handicaps, communicate with the world, and spread her lectures promoting optimism. An inspiring read for everyone... Biographies/Inspirational Pages 84

Sara Crewe *by Frances Burnett* ISBN: *1-59462-360-0* **$9.45**
In the first place, Miss Minchin lived in London. Her home was a large, dull, tall one, in a large, dull square, where all the houses were alike, and all the sparrows were alike, and where all the door-knockers made the same heavy sound... Childrens/Classic Pages 88

The Autobiography of Benjamin Franklin *by Benjamin Franklin* ISBN: *1-59462-135-7* **$24.95**
The Autobiography of Benjamin Franklin has probably been more extensively read than any other American historical work, and no other book of its kind has had such ups and downs of fortune. Franklin lived for many years in England, where he was agent... Biographies/History Pages 332

Name	
Email	
Telephone	
Address	
City, State ZIP	

☐ **Credit Card**   ☐ **Check / Money Order**

Credit Card Number	
Expiration Date	
Signature	

Please Mail to: Book Jungle
PO Box 2226
Champaign, IL 61825
or Fax to: 630-214-0564

ORDERING INFORMATION

web: *www.bookjungle.com*
email: *sales@bookjungle.com*
fax: *630-214-0564*
mail: *Book Jungle PO Box 2226 Champaign, IL 61825*
or PayPal *to sales@bookjungle.com*

Please contact us for bulk discounts

DIRECT-ORDER TERMS

**20% Discount if You Order
Two or More Books**
Free Domestic Shipping!
Accepted: Master Card, Visa,
Discover, American Express

www.ingramcontent.com/pod-product-compliance
Lightning Source LLC
Chambersburg PA
CBHW081159170626
46813CB00009B/3256